THE STORY OF FREE ENTERPRISE

THE STORY OF FREE ENTERPRISE

A Course in Basic Americanism

JOEL R. BELKNAP

Copyright © 2015 by The Devin-Adair Company, Greenwich, Connecticut.

All rights reserved. Printed in the United States of America. No part of this book may be reproduced, or stored in a retrieval system, or transmitted in any form or by any means, electronic, mechanical, photocopying, recording, or otherwise, without express written permission of the publisher.

ISBN-13: 9781517759339

CONTENTS

	Preface	vii
	Introduction to the Second Edition	xi
Chapter 1	A Land of Opportunity	1
Chapter 2	The Unalienable Rights	7
	Democracy or Republic?	22
Chapter 3	Free Enterprise	24
Chapter 4	Incentive vs. Compulsion	30
Chapter 5	Free Enterprise, Capitalism, Consumerism	39
	Intervention	39
	"The Man with the Hoe"	43
	Capitalism	44
	Consumerism	47
	Management and Labor	48
	Labor Unions	49
	Union Discipline	54
	Automation	54
	Big Business Versus Little Business	55
Chapter 6	Prosperity and Depressions	58
Chapter 7	Monopolies	68
Chapter 8	Welfare State, Socialism, Communism	76
	The Fallacy of "Federal Aid"	85
Chapter 9	Inflation—the Lure to Ruin	87
	How Inflation Works	93
Chapter 10	Socialized Security	101

Chapter 11 The Theory of Communism · 108
            American Experiments · 108
            Dialectical Materialism · 113
Chapter 12 Alternative to Socialism · 115
Chapter 13 Morality and Government · 122
            Endnotes · 133

PREFACE

OUR COUNTRY is in the forefront of a world-wide conflict. Mankind's way of life for generations to come is at stake. The conflict is variously called the "Battle For Men's Minds," the "Conflict Between Communist and Capitalist Ideologies," the "Struggle Between State Slavery and Individual Freedom," and "Individualism versus Collectivism." The present phase is described as the Cold War.

If communism continues to expand in the next ten years as it has in the last decade, all of the world's more than two and a half billion inhabitants will be within the Communist empire—with the possible exception of the United States of America. Communism has closed the Iron Curtain around 900 million people. Since 1945, Poland, Manchuria, Hungary, Bulgaria, Albania, Rumania, Czechoslovakia, China, Tibet, North Korea, the Baltic States, half of Germany, a total of some 690 million people and six million square miles of territory, have been closed in. In the Western Hemisphere, Cuba has been taken over.

Why is communism to be feared? The simple answer is, because it is evil. History has vindicated Alexis de Tocqueville's assertion that civilization depends upon a thin thread—the sanctity of contracts. Without honor between nations, foreign relations become a jungle ruled by savage force. Josef Stalin spelled out the basic tenet of Communist foreign policy this way: "Words must have no relation to actions—otherwise what kind of diplomacy is it? Words are one thing, actions another. Good words are a mask for concealment of bad deeds. Sincere diplomacy is no more possible than dry water or wooden iron."¹

Earlier, Nikolai Lenin had written: "We do not believe in eternal morality, and we expose all the fables about morality."² He could, therefore, advocate the use of any ruse, dodge, trick, cunning, unlawful method, concealment and veiling of the truth.... We must, he declared, be ready to employ trickery, deceit, law breaking, withholding and concealing truth.

Nikita Khrushchev has said: "We will bury you."³

Confronted by this savage philosophy, we depend for our survival solely upon military strength and a supposedly enlightened knowledge of communism. We see a physically powerful and ruthless empire ambitious to force its way of life on the world as it has done on its own people.

Closely related to this external danger is our internal danger—the rapid growth of paternalistic government. Election after election is won by men who extoll the "benefits" of the Welfare State. Aided by the indifference of good citizens, they have built a great bureaucracy, many of whose leaders are committed to the malignant philosophy of socialism.

They do not promote socialism as such; they enact laws that force us further down the road to socialism. Decisions of the Supreme Court extend the power of the federal government until it dominates our private lives. Soon there will be a generation that will have had no personal knowledge of the principles which built our nation into the strongest economic and political power in history.

These paternalistic measures make Communist penetration and subversion easy; Lenin predicted that America would drop like overripe fruit

---

1 Josef Stalin, quoted by Committee on Foreign Affairs, Sub-Committee No. 5, National and International Movements, "House Document No. 619," *The Strategy and Tactics of World Communism*, Supplement I, *One Hundred Years of Communism, 1848-1948* (U.S. Government Printing Office, Washington, D.C., 1948), p. 9.
2 V. I. Lenin, Address to the Young Communist League, *Ibid.*, p.73.
3 Nikita Khrushchev, Statement made during Moscow reception for Western diplomats, November 18, 1956, *Facts on File Yearbook*, 1957, p. 386.

into Communist hands. "Your grandchildren," said Khrushchev, "will be living under socialism."[4]

In the following pages we shall try to show that the original American politico-economic system had a moral philosophy which provided for the well-being of all our people.

We shall also try to show that the American system is superior to the system of state monopoly, which we discarded long ago. As a young nation, the United States sustained the right of men to think for themselves and the right to establish their own government as their servant. To preserve these rights, we must first understand them, or we are likely to sit idly by while they are destroyed before our eyes.

It is hoped that this book will teach the most important political lesson that can be learned today, which is that *the best-intentioned social reforms—no matter how humanitarian or idealistic—when executed with political power, tend to degenerate into instruments of oppression by a ruling class.*

We also hope to make it manifest that the only real security we can attain comes from opportunity to do things for ourselves under the spur of our unalienable rights. If we reject this basic American idea and accept a "government will take care of us" philosophy, all our battles for freedom from Bunker Hill to Heartbreak Hill will have been in vain.

It is all-important, in our discussion, to treat of religion. The Founding Fathers flatly forbade the establishment of any religion but guaranteed the free exercise thereof. They did not intend to promote atheism or indifference to religion. The Declaration of Independence says that governments are instituted for the purpose of securing the unalienable rights with which we are endowed by our Creator, "Nature's God." Ethics is not enough. It is a poor substitute for religious concepts. As George Washington said, ". . . reason and experience both forbid us to expect that natural morality can prevail in exclusion of religious principles."[5]

---

[4] Khrushchev, Statement made during television interview with Columbia Broadcasting System correspondents, May 28, 1957, *Ibid.*, p. 177.

[5] *The Writings of George Washington from the Original Manuscript Sources* (U.S. Government Printing Office, Washington, D.C., 1940), Vol. 35, p. 229.

Therefore, we hope to emphasize in the minds of readers the spiritual philosophy of liberty and the morality of religion; for an immoral people is incapable of self-government.

Materialism, whose logical conclusion is the Dialectical Materialism of Karl Marx, is ephemeral.

But a nation built on love of God and of our neighbor will endure. As Daniel Webster said:

> If we work upon marble, it will perish; if we work upon brass, time will efface it; if we rear temples, they will crumble into dust; but if we work upon immortal minds, if we imbue them with principles, with the just fear of God and love of our fellowmen, we engrave on those tablets something that will brighten to all eternity.[6]

This is our faith—and we believe it is a rational faith—and our guarantee of survival.

I wish to acknowledge the inspiration of the Bible and, from the great and increasing flow of libertarian literature, these books: *Human Action* by Ludwig Von Mises; *The God That Failed* by Richard Crossman; *Our Enemy the State* by Albert Jay Nock; *Man Versus the State* by Herbert Spencer; *The Road to Serfdom* by Friedrich A. Hayek; *The Return of Adam Smith* by George Montgomery.

Also the following publications: *Christian Economics; The Freeman; Human Events; College National Education Program.*

And also Mary Borden McManus for her outstanding work in checking quoted material and sources.

J. R. B.

---

6 Daniel Webster, Address in Faneuil Hall, May 22, 1852, *City Document No. 31* (J. H. Eastburn, City Printer, Boston, 1852), p. 20.

INTRODUCTION TO THE SECOND EDITION

In this thoughtful and exciting book, Joel Belknap previews our economic future and shows why the original democratic underpinnings of the American economic system are vital to our continued growth and progress.

This prescient book was originally published more than fifty years ago. It is a tribute to the author that it is as relevant today as it was then. Classics become classic because their message resonates undiminished over time. The basic principles behind *The Story of Free Enterprise* are as valid today as they were when first written.

The United States were founded as a land in which opportunity was everywhere. But to exploit the abundance and opportunity required effort and work. Success was not simply given: it had to be understood, grasped and pursued.

Belknap describes why and how the two elements of opportunity and incentive are key to American productivity.

The most powerful incentive to increased production is that the producers of goods and services control most of what they produce. They are willing to work hard and to take risks because they know, if they are successful, the rewards are theirs – not the government's.

Our American system, Belknap describes, is one that affords economic freedom to every person. American capitalism is founded upon free enterprise and liberty, whereas socialism, communism and state-limited capitalism miss these two elements.

Every American has a Constitutionally mandated, inalienable right to economic freedom. The concept of inalienable rights is the foundation of a republican government and a free enterprise system.

An economic system only works in one of two ways: the way of incentives, with a goal of profit making, or that of compulsion, backed by force and coercion.

In a system where there is no reward for individual effort, the alternative is obligation by intimidation. Fear replaces hope, quiet and sullen resentment replaces optimism, and drudgery takes the place of positive accomplishment.

Socialists and left-leaning moderates equate a free economy with greed. But that is both wrong and superficial. The motivation which runs free enterprise is self-interest, not greed. Self-interest is simply another name for legitimate incentive. Greed is excessive or reprehensible avarice (Mr. Webster's definition). Belknap recognizes that the Founders were aware of greed and the need to prevent it from undue influence in an economy. That is why the Constitution gives Congress the power to regulate commerce and trade.

Self-interest is healthy. It is an economy's lubricant; it is what people do when given opportunity. Self-interest motivates an individual and an enterprise to become more efficient and more effective. By offering better goods or services for lower prices than those of its competitors, an enterprise draws more customers or consumers to it. That builds a good reputation for the enterprise. It adds to the quality of life for others, as well as for the enterprise itself.

In short, free enterprise is a system for bringing the self-interest of people into a relationship network for providing the necessities and, yes, the luxuries which people want for improving the quality of their lives. One of the simplest ways to bankrupt a competitive enterprise is to misunderstand self-interest as greed.

In a free enterprise market, when profits of a company or an industry are positive, capital is plowed back into it, until profits diminish or cease. If the firm or the industry become overextended, low profits or losses become the rule until demand is adjusted to supply. Persons connected with a firm benefit from its prosperity. Prosperity becomes a social tool, accounting for the well-being of the community.

The competitive economy wants its customers to thrive and place a continuing flow of repeat orders. The socialist system—itself both the consumer and the producer—rations its proceeds to its customers, distributes an inordinate amount of its profits to the producing group and starves those who slow down the labor treadmill.

Belknap cites Cicero, Thomas Hobbes, Edmund Burke, Thomas Jefferson, John Stuart Mill, Abraham Lincoln when he describes the underpinnings of American democracy and economic policy.

He argues for effective checks and limits on government, no matter how benevolent the government leaders purport to be. He writes: "no dictator can rise over a people who hold the conviction that they have sacred, unalienable rights of which they cannot be deprived for any cause…" Political freedom is a guarantee and a necessity for economic freedom: they cannot be separated.

Economic freedom means that everyone has the right to buy whatever he can afford, whenever he chooses, without duress or compulsion by any government agency. This is as true of health care and liquor as it is of bread and water.

The power of private incentives versus directed socialism, the effects of monopolies, the weaknesses of the welfare bureaucracy, the morality of free choice, the fallacies behind federal aid are all analyzed and described in simple terms and clear examples.

Read this book! Reflect on its importance in today's economy. Heed its advice to assure a richer world for tomorrow!

Roger H. Lourie, Publisher
Greenwich, Connecticut
2015

Chapter One
A Land of Opportunity

Only one in every 20 babies brought into the world is born in the United States of America. Thirteen of the 20 are born in extreme poverty. They will live in thatched huts with dirt floors and will suffer hunger and disease.

We have poverty in America, but the poorest of us enjoys advantages far greater than does the average person of any other land. A man and his wife, though unskilled, can accumulate enough property with industry and thrift to rear their children decently and support themselves in old age.

The great majority of us accept as ordinary such conveniences as bathtubs, hot and cold water, modern plumbing, radios, and automobiles. We attend school and can go to college if we qualify and wish to do so.

Our high standard of living has been accomplished despite the waste of two immensely costly world wars and billions of dollars in goods to subsidize industries in nations stifled by government controls, socialism, communism, and underdevelopment.

We take our standard of living as a matter of course; it is a perfectly natural right, for it has been earned. It is a product of individual freedom under justice. This freedom is under constant attack; our defense of it is endless, requiring eternal vigilance.

Our Constitution did more than create a union of states. It established justice, insured domestic tranquility, provided for the national defense, promoted the general welfare and, greatest of all, guaranteed the blessings of liberty and economic freedom to all citizens equally under the law.* With such safeguards, a free economic system took root and flourished as in no other land.

In Lincoln's day, the country lay midway between its early birthpains and its present maturity. A dominant role in world affairs was undreamed of. People succeeded by their own efforts, and the rest of the world was left to do the same. Freedom and equal opportunities were the government's only guarantees to its citizens. Promises of economic security now have been added. Great numbers of individuals are supported by the government, yet the sole support of the government still is the people.

It is the freedoms on which this country was founded that have made it great. We have done more with what we have than other countries have done. We have a fair share of the world's natural resources—minerals, arable land, and water power. Also we have mass production methods. Eli Whitney devised modern mass production with his cotton gin more than a hundred years ago. We hold no secrets, no patents on production methods.

A primitive form of mass production was devised in the fifteenth century, when Venice created the assembly line. What was then the world's largest industrial plant, known as the Arsenal, built ships and nails and cannons. It produced a standardized craft that could be quickly converted from merchant ship to war galley. The hull was launched and towed slowly along a narrow canal. Workmen loaded on equipment from windows in buildings on both sides. When it reached the end of the canal, it was equipped with oars, armament, food, cargo, and crew.

"In this manner," a Spanish visitor wrote in 1436, "ten fully equipped galleys came out in six hours." In the 1570 war with the Turks, the Arsenal outfitted a hundred galleys in a hundred days.

Watches and clocks replaced sundials and hour glasses centuries ago. They remained a cumbersome luxury until a jeweler in Elgin, Illinois, devised machine-made standardized parts.

Representatives of foreign governments and industry, including those from Communist countries, inspect our factories and study our methods. The Soviet Union confiscated several factories of the International Harvester Company when it nationalized all industry in that country. When production collapsed, the American company was asked to manage the factories for the government. The company refused, but it offered to train future foremen sent from Russia. Also, the company gave blueprints and models of its latest tractors and farm machines to Moscow.

"People may think we're crazy," the late Alexander Legge, president of the company, said. "The fact is that we'll have new models and better methods, and the others will be obsolete by the time the Russians get into production."[1]

No nation has a monopoly on science or technology. The steam engine, the steam turbine, the internal-combustion engine, the locomotive, the jet plane were invented in foreign lands. Russia launched an earth satellite before we did. Many industrial processes, such as synthetic rubber, have been invented by citizens of other countries. Vaccination, pasteurization, and many valuable drugs have originated abroad.

But, on the whole, the inventions and scientific discoveries of foreign citizens find a more fertile field in America, with quicker and greater rewards, than in their own countries. We have imported many inventions and scientific discoveries, put them to commercial use, and improved them by continual experimenting and testing.

Two-thirds of the people of the earth go to bed hungry every night, yet the countries in which they live have a much higher proportion of farmers than we do. The percentage of population necessary to provide food for a nation is a good measure of its material progress. Some "backward" nations require that half or more of their people work on food production.

Since 1914, farm laborers in the United States have declined from 12,000,000 to about 5,000,000. Over the same period, with only one percent more land in cultivation, farm production has practically doubled. Production per worker has increased two and a half times through machinery and improved methods, in spite of fewer hours of work.

The American farmer not only produces enough food for the United States; he is subsidized to produce a surplus, which the government gives or sells at low prices to less fortunate countries.

---

[1] Alexander Legge, Letter to Mary Borden McManus from John W. Vance, International Harvester Co., Chicago, August 29, 1962.

JOEL R. BELKNAP

A typical family market basket has been put together by the U.S. Bureau of Labor Statistics to show how well the American family lives. It contains these foods:

Round Steak, 3 lbs.
Sugar, 5 lbs.
Bacon, 2 lbs.
Lard, pound
Eggs, dozen
Bread, loaf
Butter, pound
Milk, quart
Coffee, pound
Oranges, dozen
Cabbage, 3 lbs.
Potatoes, peck
Corn, can
Peas, can
Tomatoes, can

The contents may vary as to family tastes and seasons. Prices also vary from month to month. But, averaging everything out, in this country the head of a family works one minute less than 5 hours to earn the price of this typical basket of food. In Canada, he works 6½ hours; in Great Britain, 8½ hours; in France, 15 hours, 39 minutes, and in the Soviet Union 38 hours, 27 minutes.

In the Soviet Union, where government dictation is absolute, a man works 8 *days* to buy a pair of shoes, compared to 5½ *hours* in the United States; 4 hours, 8 minutes for a pound of beef, compared to 26 minutes; 2 hours, 48 minutes for a dozen eggs, compared to 21 minutes, and proportionately for other necessities.

The severe living conditions are partly accounted for by diversion of labor and resources to projects which the ruling class considers more desirable than raising the standard of living—armaments, public works, space probes, and luxuries for themselves. Beef and dairy cattle in the Soviet

Union numbered only 56,000,000 head in 1953, compared to 58,400,000 in 1916 under the Czar and 66,800,000 in 1928, after Lenin. Grain crops also have decreased until, today, this vast agricultural country does not produce enough food for its own people. In Commnist China and East Germany, severe food shortages are developing, while Americans are better fed than any other nation on earth. Because the food supply was low in France and England after the war, our agricultural experts told them they needed more machines on the farms." So we provided more horsepower for the French and English farms.

The food supply increased very little, and the farm machinery seemed to create more unemployment. What happened was that the economy, "stabilized" by government controls, did not stabilize.

The marginal farmer was eliminated for the most part in America by the tractor, hybrid corn, better fertilizers and grasses, and cattle that produce twice as much milk and beef as those of fifty years ago. We have hens that are more productive each succeeding year, thoroughbred pigs, and scientific control of plant and animal diseases.

It becomes obvious, then, that we have an abundance of food because we produce more with an hour of labor than does any other nation on earth.

We have an abundance of *all* things because we produce them in abundance. We have more than other nations because we produce more.

The reason is that we have a basic impelling force that makes men willing to work to produce so much. They have opportunity and incentive. The most powerful incentive is the fact that the producers have been permitted to keep control of a large share of what they produce. They are willing to work, to think, and to take the risks of costly experiments. They do not only produce an abundance, they develop and create entirely new things.

Our standard of living is still advancing, in spite of heavy taxes to meet huge appropriations for defense against the threat of Communist aggression and in spite of socialization on a large scale.

We call our economic system "free enterprise," "free capitalism," or simply "capitalism," as distinguished from the state capitalism of socialism and communism. Whatever the designation, we mean a system that affords economic freedom to every citizen.

And every man has an *unalienable right* to economic freedom. The concept of unalienable rights is fundamental to a republican government and a free economic system.

We shall consider now the nature of unalienable rights and why we are entitled to them.

Chapter Two
THE UNALIENABLE RIGHTS

The Government of the United States of America is founded on the premise that all men are born with certain sacred and unalienable rights that no one, even a government, can rightly take away. The political foundations of many other nations are based on the theory that all rights are vested in a government that grants certain privileges to the people. Under the American Constitution, the government has only such rights as are delegated to it by the people. Therefore, the government cannot have rights that the people do not have.

This principle, which assures individual freedom and makes government subordinate to the people, is laid down in the second paragraph of the Declaration of Independence:

> We hold these truths to be self-evident, that all men are created equal, that they are endowed by their Creator with certain unalienable Rights, that among these are Life, Liberty, and the pursuit of Happiness. That to secure these rights, Governments are instituted among Men, deriving their just powers from the consent of the governed. That whenever any form of Government becomes destructive of these ends, it is the Right of the People to alter or to abolish it, and to institute new Government, laying its foundation on such principles and organizing its powers in such form, as to them shall seem most likely to effect their Safety and Happiness.

That mankind has unalienable rights was not new as a theory, though it had never been admitted by a government.

> True law [said Cicero] is right reason in agreement with nature; it is of universal application, unchanging and everlasting; it summons to duty by its commands, and averts from wrongdoing by its prohibitions. . . . We cannot be freed from its obligations by senate or people, and we need not look outside ourselves for an expounder or interpreter of it. And there will not be different laws, at Rome and at Athens, or different laws now and in the future, but one eternal and unchangeable law will be valid for all nations and all times, . . . Whoever is disobedient is fleeing from himself and denying his human nature, . . ."[1]

In 1651 Thomas Hobbes wrote in *Leviathan:*

> Princes succeed one another; and one judge passeth, another cometh; nay, heaven and earth shall pass, for it is the eternal law of God. Therefore all the sentences of precedent judges that have ever been cannot altogether make a law contrary to natural equity.[2]

And Edmund Burke (1729-1797) said:

> There is but one law for all; namely, the law that governs all law—the law of our Creator.[3]

Human beings receive an inherent dignity, self-respect, and code of righteousness from a higher power. The individual sense of right and wrong, the conscience, controls human conduct more basically than do all laws. Good citizens shun those persons whose practice is to stay within the letter of the law while violating the common principles of fair play. Honesty is inherent in orderly society.

---

1 C. W. Keyes, *Cicero: De Re Publica* (Loeb Library, Harvard University Press, Cambridge, Massachusetts, 1948), p. 211.
2 Thomas Hobbes, *Leviathan* (The Liberal Arts Press, New York, 1958), Part II, p. 220.
3 Edmund Burke, quoted by Burton Stevenson (ed.), *The Home Book of Quotations* (Dodd, Mead & Co., New York, 1958), p. 1083.

This does not mean that the unwritten law of the jungle protects individual rights. Representatives of orderly government must enact laws or regulations forbidding acts by an individual which interfere with the rights or peaceful lives of others. Economic freedom, for example, is an unalienable right; but if it is carried so far by a person in practice as to make it impossible for others to enjoy their own economic freedom, laws must be brought into play to limit that person's activity; hence the Sherman Anti-Trust Act. Certain rights are enumerated in the Constitution and twenty-eight are specified in the first ten amendments to that basic law—the Bill of Rights. The Ninth Amendment says: "The enumeration in the Constitution, of certain rights, shall not be construed to deny or disparage others retained by the people."

Today, we retain and exercise these individual rights as a matter of course.

Those who signed the Declaration of Independence on July 4, 1776, and the Constitution eleven years later, were exultant over their newly won freedom. As in all legislatures, more than half were lawyers. Next in number were merchants, farmers, soldiers, and physicians; there was a clergyman, a professor, a printer, a musician, a brewer. The delegates were familiar with the early failures of government autocracy, public ownership, and planned economy in the Virginia and New England colonies. They had leisure to read and weigh the philosophies of others, and by independent reasoning seem to have arrived at a common philosophy.

This philosophy was summarized in an old proverb of Virginia: "That government is best that governs least."[4] And again by Thomas Jefferson, farmer, lawyer, statesman, and original do-it-yourself American:

> If we can prevent the government from wasting the labors of the people under the pretense of taking care of them, they must become happy.[5]

---

4 *The Free Enterpriser* (Arkansas Free Enterprise Association, Little Rock, Arkansas, September 1952), p. 3.
5 John P. Foley (ed.), *The Jeffersonian Cyclopedia* (Funk 8c Wagnalls Co., New York and London, 1900), p. 459.

The Virginia Bill of Rights, which antedated the Declaration of Independence by a few weeks, states the case for the unalienable rights:

> All men are by nature equally free and independent, and have certain inherent rights, of which, when they enter into a state of society, they cannot by any compact deprive or divest their posterity: namely, the enjoyment of life and liberty, with the means of acquiring and possessing property, and pursuing and obtaining happiness and safety.[6]

Freedom is the unhampered right to express opinions, own property, travel, work, play, and pursue the opportunities of life. It includes the right to follow one's own economic, religious, and political tendencies. Freedom is indivisible; when we lose the exercise of freedom in one category, we lose it in all.

While freedom is an unhampered right, it has to be curbed when it infringes upon the freedom of others, or it becomes license. The curbing of some freedoms assures the greatest freedom to the greatest number. A man is not free to tear up railroad tracks, because in so doing he eliminates the freedom of others to travel. He is not free to murder or steal, because he thereby deprives another of life or the freedom to enjoy the fruits of his industry. Countless laws in every free country protect the rights of the individual. Even without specific laws, men of good intention do not trespass on the rights of others.

Ignazio Silone, an ex-Communist, expressed the American principle of freedom when he said:

> Liberty is the possibility of doubting, the possibility of making a mistake, the possibilty of searching and experimenting, the possibility of saying "No" to any authority—literary, artistic, philosophic, religious, social and even political.[7]

---

6 James Morton Smith and James Murphy (eds.), *Liberty and Justice, A Historical Record of American Constitutional Development* (Alfred A. Knopf, Inc., New York, 1958), p. 50.

7 Ignazio Silone, quoted by Richard Crossman, *The God That Failed* (Harper & Bros., New York, 1949), p. 102.

Does freedom of speech and press mean freedom to say or print what we please, regardless of truth? The answer is supplied by Dr. Kenneth W. Sollitt:

> Freedom is never license to do as we please but only freedom to do as we ought, and that freedom is only for those who accept the responsibilities that go along with it.[8]

True freedom can never interfere with the duties, rights, and interests of others, and while the individual in a republic is prohibited from interfering with the rights and opportunities of others, his own freedom to increase his stature and welfare is infinite.

The only freedom that a man can demand is freedom to have all restrictions removed that prevent his doing what he has a moral right to do.

> Where the spirit of the Lord is, there is liberty.—11 Corinthians 3:17.

> The God who gave us life gave us liberty at the same time.[9]—Thomas Jefferson (1743-1826).

> Natural liberty is the gift of the beneficent Creator to the whole human race, and . . . civil liberty is founded in that.[10]—Alexander Hamilton, in "The Farmer Refuted." 1775.

> Stand fast therefore in the liberty wherewith Christ made us free, and be not entangled again with the yoke of bondage.—Galatians 5:1.

John Stuart Mill explained the nature of liberty in these words:

> To prevent the weaker members of a community from being preyed upon by innumerable vultures, it was needful that there should be an

---

8 Kenneth W. Sollitt, quoted in *Congressional Record*, Appendix, inserted by the Hon. Norris Paulson, September 28, 1951, p. A6266, col. 3.
9 Foley, *op. cit.*, p. 500.
10 Alexander Hamilton, quoted by Saul K. Padover, *The Mind of Alexander Hamilton* (Harper & Bros., New York, 1958), p. 88.

animal of prey stronger than the rest, commissioned to keep them down. But as the king of the vultures would be no less bent upon preying upon the flock than any of the minor harpies, it was indispensable to be in a perpetual attitude of defense against his beak and claws. The end, therefore, of patriots was to set limits to the power which the ruler should be suffered to exercise over the community; and this limitation was what they meant by liberty.[11]

After the right to life itself, the most important of Unalienable Rights is the right to liberty.

The Declaration first specified the right to life, then liberty. Many people value liberty even more than life, for what value has life without liberty?

Give me liberty or give me death.[12]—Patrick Henry.

We would rather die on our feet than live on our knees.—Spanish proverb.

The Founders of the Republic lived in the age of kings who justified their despotic laws by "divine right." The Founding Fathers realized that government, though necessary and a source of great good, could be the worst enemy of the people's freedom if its activities were not restricted. They knew that mankind's struggle for freedom was always a struggle against government.

Many people believed that royalty was responsible for war and oppression; all that was necessary to put an end to these was to abolish royalty. The Founders knew that the cause lay deeper—*in government itself, of which kings and queens might be only symbols.*

---

11 John Stuart Mill, "Essay on Liberty" quoted by George Seldes, *The Great Quotations* (Lyle Stuart, New York, 1960), p. 490.
12 Patrick Henry, Speech in Virginia Convention, March 23, 1775, quoted by John Bartlett (ed.), *Familiar Quotations* (Little, Brown & Co., Boston, 1937), p. 270.

Other statesmen and scholars have voiced the same philosophy of liberty:

> "Man is born free and everywhere he is in chains.—Jean Jacques Rousseau."[13]

John Locke, an Englishman who died in 1704, wrote his two *Treatises on Civil Government* almost a century before the American Revolution. His volume was in the libraries of statesmen and undoubtedly had a profound influence on those who drafted the Declaration of Independence and our Constitution. He expounded the unalienable rights of men to rule themselves:

> The natural liberty of man is to be free from any superior power on earth, and not to be under the will or legislative authority of man, but to have only the law of nature for his rule. The liberty of man, in society is to be under no other legislative power, but that established by consent in the commonwealth; nor under the dominion of any will or restraint of any law, but what that legislative power shall enact according to the trust put in it. . . .[14]
>
> However it may be mistaken, the end of law is, not to abolish or restrain, but to preserve and enlarge freedom. For in all the states of created beings capable of laws, where there is no law there is no freedom. For liberty is to be free from restraint and violence from others; which cannot be where there is no law: and is not, as we are told, a liberty for every man to do what he lists. (For who could be free when every other man's humor might domineer over him?) But a liberty to dispose, and order as he lists, his person, actions, possessions, and his whole property, within the allowance of those laws under which he is, and therein

---

13 Jean Jacques Rousseau, quoted by Norman L. Torrey (ed.), *Les Philosophes* (Capricorn Books, New York, 1960), p. 144.
14 John Locke, quoted in *The Christian Origin of the Constitution of the United States* (American Principle, Inc., The Advance Printing Co., San Francisco, California), p. 63.

not to be subject to the arbitrary will of another, but freely follow his own.[15]

Men being, as has been said, by nature all free, equal, and independent, no one can be put out of this estate, and subjected to the political power of another, without his own consent. The only way by which any divests himself of his natural liberty and puts on the bonds of civil society is by agreeing with other men to join and unite into a community for their comfortable, safe, and peaceable living one amongst another, in a secure enjoyment of their properties, and a greater security against any that are not of it. This any number of men may do, because it injures not the freedom of the rest; they are left as they were in the liberty of the state of nature.[16]

... And thus that which begins and actually constitutes any political society is nothing but the consent of any number of freemen capable of a majority to unite and incorporate into such a society. And this is that, and that only, which did or could give beginning to any lawful government in the world. [17]

Inscribed on the Liberty Bell in Philadelphia, which sounded freedom for the new nation, is a verse of Leviticus XXV: 10: "And proclaim liberty throughout the land and to all the inhabitants thereof."

Freedom endures because it is born in the hearts of mankind. It was suppressed for ages, and dictators and governments may only briefly usurp it today. It is a human instinct that cannot be killed.

In his inaugural address in 1801, Thomas Jefferson said:

Still one thing more, fellow citizens, to make us a happy and prosperous people: A wise and frugal government which shall restrain men from injuring one another, which shall leave them otherwise free to regulate their own pursuits of industry and improvement and shall not take from the mouth of labor the bread it has

---

15 *The Works of John Locke* (Thomas Davidson, London, 1823), Vol. V, pp. 94-95.
16 *Ibid.*, p. 394.
17 *Ibid.*, p. 396.

earned ... Equal and exact justice to all men ... Economy in the public expense, that labor may be lightly burdened; the honest payment of our debts and the sacred preservation of public faith: encouragement of agriculture and of commerce its handmaid; the diffusion of public information and the arraignment of all abuses at the bar of public reason; freedom of religion, freedom of the press; ... these principles form the bright constellation which has gone before us. ... They should be the creed of our political faith, the text of civil instruction, the touchstone by which to try the services of those we trust.[18]

More than half a century later, Abraham Lincoln declared:

The principles of Jefferson are the definitions and axioms of a free society. Our reliance is in the love of liberty which God has implanted in us. Our defense is in the spirit which prizes liberty as the heritage of all men, in all lands, everywhere.[19]

Another half century passed and another president (and historian), Woodrow Wilson, affirmed the same truth:

Liberty has never come from government. Liberty has always come from subjects of it. The history of liberty is the history of limitations of governmental power, not in increase of it. ... When we resist the concentration of governmental power, we resist the processes of death, because a concentration of governmental power is what always precedes the death of human liberty.[20]

---

18 Thomas Jefferson, quoted by William Ebenstein, *Two Ways of Life, The Communist Challenge to Democracy* (Holt, Rinehart & Winston, Inc., New York, 1962), p. 364.
19 Abraham Lincoln, Letter to H. L. Pierce and others, April 16, 1850, Roy P. Basler (ed.), *Abraham Lincoln, His Speeches and Writing* (The World Publishing Co., Cleveland and New York, 1946), p. 488.
20 Woodrow Wilson, Address to New York Press Club, May 19, 1912, quoted by Seldes, *op. cit.*, p. 750.

Humble people as well as great have proclaimed the same faith in liberty. The Committee on un-American Activities of the House of Representatives said in 1939:

> Americanism is the recognition of the truth that the inherent and fundamental rights of man are derived from God and not from governments.[21]

The Natural Law Institute, with believers in Buddhism, Confucianism, Judaism, Islam, and Christianity, met at Notre Dame University under Clarence E. Manion, a former dean of the Law School there. Differing widely in creeds, they affirmed the doctrine of our nation's forefathers that truth, justice, and honor are natural moral forces which man-made laws should support and never attempt to supplant.

The destructive material and political conflicts between Libertarian, Socialist, and Communist worlds all spring from their doctrinal differences on the human rights of man. The theories differ on whether man is a superior being or a species of dumb animal. One theory leads to harmony among people, the other to rivalry and destruction.

The Founders' theory holds that man is an image of his Creator, crowned with glory and honor and given dominion over all things, but *not* over other men. But the Socialists and Communists promulgate a very different theory: man is "another excrescence in an enormous and heartless cosmos, crawling on a rock that spins through space." As in other forms of life, animate and inanimate, men are doomed to struggle with one another for survival. For political profit, this theory, denying the intelligence of man, is offered to the proletariat with the promise that they will emerge as the victors.

Socialism and communism rest on the doctrine that the state is supreme and that the individual does not have inherent rights:

---

[21] House Committee on un-American Activities, *Annual Report*, January 3, 1939, p. 10.

"No rights are absolute"; and "Liberty" is what the party permits just as "truth" is whatever the party line happens to be. "Human rights" become grudging doles of party patronage.

"Marxism is materialism," wrote Lenin. "We must combat individualism and, most of all, religion."[22] Obedience to changing dogma formulated by party dictators is enforced, and independent thought is forbidden.

Louis Fischer, disillusioned by his years in what he had extolled as the Soviet Utopia, wrote:

> *There is no freedom in a dictatorship because there are no unalienable rights.* The dictator has so much power and the individual so little that the dictator can take away any right which he gives. The "right to work," for instance, today may mean in a factory for pay and tomorrow grim necessity in a concentration camp for starvation rations. The citizen has no redress, for the dictator is the legislator, the executive and the judge. The hardworking and talented Soviet people deserve better and know better, but they cannot help themselves and each year the terror increases.[23]
>
> [author's italics]

A man's unalienable rights include the material right to property and profits, freedom from aggression, and the abstract right to form his own opinions and have a voice in government.

Justice Brandeis ruled:

> They [the authors of the Constitution] conferred as against the government) the right to be let alone—the most comprehensive of rights, and the right most valued by civilized man.[24]

---

22 V. I. Lenin as quoted in *Soviet World Outlook*, prepared by Division of Research for USSR and Eastern Europe, Office of Intelligence Research, Department of State, for the Coordinator of Psychological Intelligence, U.S. Information Agency, 1954, p. 185.
23 Louis Fischer, quoted by Crossman, *op. cit.*, p. 225.
24 Mr. Justice Brandeis dissenting opinion in Olmstead *et al. v.* United States, Green *et al. v.* United States, and McInnis *v.* United States, 277, 277 U.S. 438, p. 478.

No individual has the right to steal another person's property. Nor does the government have a right to take a man's property or profits without compensation. That unalienable right is being nibbled away, as we shall see in a later chapter.

From thousands of years of recorded history, the Founders knew that it is in the nature of governments to expand, to live by the creation of privileges for groups or classes; they therefore dedicated the new government to equality of rights under which special privileges were to be abolished. All citizens were to have equal opportunities. The essence of government, to them, was the task of safeguarding this equality and limiting the powers of government. Amendment X says, "The powers not delegated to the United States by the Constitution, nor prohibited to it by the States, are reserved to the States respectively or to the people." The rights of freedom of speech and press were emphasized. And yet, shortly before he died on July 4 1826, Jefferson wrote:

> I see with the deepest affliction the rapid strides with which the Federal branch of our government is advancing toward the usurpation of all the rights reserved to the States, and the consolidation in itself of all powers, domestic and foreign; and that, too, by constructions which, if legitimate, leave no limits to their power.[25]

William Henry Chamberlin observes:

> The influence of this theory of natural rights—an attribute of every human being, which is not within the lawful power of any human being to curtail or withhold—on successive generations of Americans is almost incalculable. It still remains the best shield against the materialistic conception of modern dictatorships.[26]

No dictator can rise over a people who hold the conviction that they have sacred, unalienable rights of which they cannot be deprived for any cause

---

25 Foley, *op. cit.*, p. 132.
26 William Henry Chamberlain, Letter to Mary Borden McManus, August 31, 1962.

whatever, by any man or group of men, by power seekers or benefactors who would destroy or abridge these rights "to promote the general welfare." Political freedom is a guarantee of economic freedom; the two are inseparable.

The Founders of the Republic believed unshakably that, unless firmly restricted, centralized government creates tyranny. They would undoubtedly have agreed that today's benevolent government is sure to be tomorrow's despotism unless effective limits and checks are placed on its power.

In No. 47 of *The Federalist*, James Madison said:

> The accumulation of all powers, legislative, executive and judiciary, in the same hands, whether of one, a few or many, and whether hereditary, self-appointed or elective, may justly be pronounced the very definition of tyranny.[27]

And Jefferson:

> Were not this great country already divided into states, that division must be made, that each might do for itself what concerns itself directly, and what it can so much better do than a distant authority. Every state again is divided into counties, each to take care of what lies within its local bounds; each county again into townships or wards, to manage minuter details: and every ward into farms, to be governed each by its individual proprietor. . . . It is by this partition of cares, descending in gradation from general to particular, that the mass of human affairs may be best managed for the good and prosperity of all.[28]

Charles Louis de Secondet Montesquieu, a French philosopher who lived from 1689 to 1755, wrote the "Spirit of Laws" in 1734. By 1789, when the American Constitutional Convention began, the "Spirit of Laws" had

---

[27] James Madison, *The Federalist* (Modern Library Edition, Random House, New York), p. 313.
[28] Foley, *op. cit.*, p. 424.

become a classic. Reference was made to it frequently in the Constitutional debates. Montesquieu advocated the tripartite separation of government into Executive, Judiciary, and Legislative branches. He considered the Judiciary to be the weakest of the three. Alexander Hamilton, citing Montesquieu, observed:

> The Judiciary . . . has no influence over the sword or the purse; no direction either of the strength or of the wealth of the society; and can take no active resolution whatever. It may truly be said to have neither FORCE NOR WILL, but merely judgement; and must ultimately depend upon the aid of the executive arm even for the efficacy of its judgements.[29]

He also said, with Montesquieu, that "there is no liberty, if the power of judging be not separated from the Legislative and Executive powers."[30] Montesquieu observed (as quoted by Madison):

> When the legislative and executive powers are united in the same person or body, . . . there can be no liberty, because apprehensions may arise lest the same monarch or senate should enact tyrannical laws, to execute them in a tyrannical manner.

> Were the power of judging joined with the legislative, the life and liberty of the subject would be exposed to arbitrary control, for the judge would then be the legislator. Were it joined to the executive power, the judge might behave with all the violence of an oppressor.[31]

Hamilton further declared:

> . . . the whole power of raising armies was lodged in the *Legislature*, not the Executive; . . .

---

29 Alexander Hamilton, *The Federalist*, p. 504.
30 *Ibid.*
31 James Madison, *The Federalist*, p. 315.

> The remaining powers which the plan of the convention allots to the Senate, in a distinct capacity, are comprised in their participation with the executive in the appointment to offices, . . .[32]

The Founders regarded division of the powers of government as the first line of the defense of liberty. They devised a government that could check and balance itself with three divisions, Legislative, Executive and Judicial. It was to be, intentionally, deliberative and cumbersome—and ever since has been the despair of those who want immediate government action. When men want our government to act hastily, they usually appeal through the president. Ambitious presidents have found ways to expand their powers until, today, the Executive overbears the Legislative and the Judicial, at times virtually monopolizing the government.

In his Farewell Address, George Washington solemnly warned us:

> The spirit of encroachment tends to consolidate the powers of all the departments into one, and thus create, whatever the form of government, a real despotism. A just estimate of that love of power and proneness to abuse it which predominates in the human heart is sufficient to satisfy us of the truth of this position. The necessity of reciprocal checks in the exercise of political power, by dividing and distributing it in different depositories, and constituting each the guardian of the public weal, against invasions by others, has been evinced by experiments ancient and modern: some of them in our country and under our own eyes. To preserve them must be as necessary as to institute them.

By contrast, Louis Fischer, in *The God That Failed* portrays the monolithic Soviet government:

> Russia is condemned as a "police state." That is a fraction of the evil. The Kremlin holds its citizens in subjugation not only by police and prison power but also by the greater power inherent in the ownership

---

32 Hamilton, *The Federalist*, pp. 148,423.

and operation of every economic enterprise in the nation. . . . There is no appeal from its might, because there is no power in the Soviet Union that does not belong to the dictatorship.[33]

Democracy or Republic?

Our country is sometimes called a democracy. The Greeks gave us the word "democracy," which means "rule by the people." "Democracy" is not found in either the Declaration of Independence or the Constitution. Article IV of the Constitution provides that "The United States shall guarantee to every state in the union a Republican form of government."

In a democracy, the majority is the government, and the minority is at its mercy. It is a numbers game, in which 51% is the winner and 49% the loser; in some cases, an arbitrary two-thirds is the winner. James Madison distinguished sharply between republics and democracies:

> Democracies have ever been spectacles of turbulence and contention; have ever been found incompatible with personal security or the rights of property; and have in general been as short in their lives as they have been violent in their deaths.[34]

Nearly one hundred years ago, the British essayist Thomas Babington Macaulay expressed serious apprehension over the elements of democracy in our government:

> I have long been convinced that institutions purely Democratic must sooner or later destroy liberty, or civilization or both. . . .[35]

---

33 Louis Fischer, quoted by Crossman, *op. cit.*, p. 226-7.
34 Madison, *The Federalist*, p. 58.
35 Thomas Babington Macaulay, Letter to an American Friend, May 23, 1875, quoted by Seldes, *op. cit.*, p. 452-3.

"Republic," from the Latin *respublica*, meaning "of interest to the public," signifies representative government, founded on a limiting constitution. Our republic has a tripartite division of federal authority, with state and individual rights clearly defined.

In 1935, the Communist International met in Moscow and decreed that the Soviet Union should henceforth be described as a "democracy." Communist-front organizations throughout the world have since incorporated the words "democracy" or "democratic" in their titles. Communist countries call themselves "people's democracies." They have endeavored to make the words "communism" and "democracy" synonymous. When Josef Stalin died in March 1953, the National Committee of the Communist Party in the United States called his passing "a heavy loss to the Soviet people, as well as to the toiling masses and all the forces of peace, democracy and Socialism throughout the world,"[36] thereby linking democracy with socialism.

---

36 *Political Affairs*, March 1953, p. 6.

Chapter Three
FREE ENTERPRISE

Economic freedom, as we have said, is an unalienable right. Loss of that freedom means slavery.

Individual economic freedom necessitates a free economic system; in fact, a free economy is the sum of individual freedoms. It can exist only when individuals are free to exchange the fruits of their industry at the best prices they can obtain, and buy the goods and services of others most advantageously. The individual must compete with others when he sells; only then will he enable others to compete in selling to him.

A free economic system, therefore, is one that is free of political control except to establish justices so that men may be prevented from injuring one another. It assures a free market, one that is not influenced by cartels, monopolies, price-fixing, production controls, dishonest money and inflation, or tariffs. A free market accurately sums up the influences of all individuals on supply and demand so that they can determine what is to be produced, how much, when, and at what prices. Economic freedom means that everyone shall have the right to buy whatever he wants, wherever he chooses, at his own good pleasure, without duress or compulsion by the government or by any other agency.

His dollar of expenditure is his vote. As Max Eastman puts it:

> When a man buys something on a free market, he is casting his vote as a citizen of the national economy. He is making a choice which, by influencing prices, will enter into the decision as to how, and toward what

ends, the economy shall be conducted . . . the market makes freedom possible in a complex industrial society.[1]

Thomas Jefferson outlined economic freedom this way:

> The first principle of association [human society] is the guarantee to everyone of a free exercise of his industry and the possession of the fruits acquired by it.[2]

The theory of economic freedom worked well for a hundred and fifty years and built a great nation. Now we are diverging from its principles. One group after another—the educator, the farmer, the airline, the railroad—demands government aid or special privileges to obtain "fair prices" or "fair wages" or perhaps a "free" or nearly "free" pension. In so doing, they seek to substitute political distribution of wealth for fair economic distribution. Throughout history, political distribution of wealth has resulted in financial possession of all wealth by a ruling class.

The finished product of one trade is the raw material of another. Government interference to raise or lower prices may help this or that group for a time, but only if money is taken from another group; and a great part will be taken in transit, as toll, by the bureaucracy. The government is robbing Peter to pay Paul for his vote and charging the public a high commission for the job.

Communists, Socialists, and our home-grown Collectivists denounce competition as "law of the claw and fang, dog eat dog, devil take the hindmost."

Everything is devouring something and in turn is being devoured, in a jungle fight for survival.

The collectivist says that cooperation is a higher principle, more productive, more economical, and more humane. His arguments are

---

[1] Max Eastman, *Reflections on the Failure of Socialism* (The Devin-Adair Co., New York, 1955), p. 32.
[2] John P. Foley (ed.), *The Jeffersonian Cyclopedia* (Funk & Wagnalls Co., New York and London, 1900), p. 424.

presented in alluring language. Even scholarly works sometimes tend to give this impression.

The *Standard International Encyclopedia* gives this definition of socialism:

> A theory of social organization which aims to reorganize society on the basis of cooperation rather than competition.

The Soviet Union is a shining example of collectivism, but not of cooperation. Soviet apologists shut their eyes to the causative chain that converted the Soviet's "intelligent control" into a ruthless police state, enforcing its rule by the execution of millions and by banishments to slave-labor camps. When they speak of cooperation, they mean regimentation and compulsion. In a free competitive economy, cooperation is voluntary and real.

Competition can be fair or unfair, civilized or savage, cooperative or noncooperative. Rivals can destroy each other, but then competition is a failure. Or they can cooperate, and the resulting competition stimulates both rivals to greater effort. Cooperation, tolerance, love and respect for one's fellowmen make successful competition. Henry Clay said, when the nation was young:

> By competition, the total amount of the supply is increased, and by increase of the supply a competition in the sale ensues, and this enables the consumer to buy at lower rates. Of all human powers operating on the affairs of mankind, none is greater than that of competition.[3]

And Dr. James B. Conant observed a century later, when he was president of Harvard, that progress depends on competition. Justice Louis Brandeis of the Supreme Court, wrote further, in an opinion, that regulating and restricting competition would be like substituting a monarchy for a republic.

---

3 Richard Chambers, *Speeches of the Hon. Henry Clay of the Congress of the United States* (Shepard & Sterns, Cincinnati, Ohio, 1842), p. 187.

Reginald Balmforth, an English writer, drawing comparisons between primitive and civilized man and between shifty and fair commercial practices, said that those with the higher moral standards and those motivated by intelligence and brotherly love, tend to survive those more selfish and less intelligent.

Collectivists denounce competition as a waste. Advertising, for example, is a useless expense in merchandising, they say. But this is another Marxist-Leninist theory which experience proves to be false. Advertising is information; it informs people about new services and products, thereby helping to create a demand. The demand is reflected in more purchases, these result in greater production and, consequently, in greater wealth. Even in the Soviet Union, where competition has been abolished, the government advertises the little that is in the stores to inform the people.

Again, it is argued that distribution costs are high. Often it costs more than the cost of manufacture to get an article from the factory into the hands of the consumer. But the cost of distribution is actually brought down by competition. Supermarkets have reduced the cost of food distribution as much as 40% in some localities. New methods of packaging, storing, handling, transporting, and selling merchandise are constantly being tested.

Competition can be an orderly game or a bloody riot. Fair umpiring is necessary, and is the proper task of government, in accord with the basic American principle that "men should be restrained from injuring one another, otherwise free." Our great corporations, cooperatives, and partnerships "farm-out" tremendous lots of work to smaller enterprises, thereby keeping these healthy and thriving. We ought to know about cooperation.

The organizing of a football team calls for as many candidates as possible for each position. If there are enough, there might be two or more teams, or a team of "scrubs" against which to train the varsity team. A competitor is "breathing down the neck" of every boy who may feel too sure of his position on the varsity team. Healthy competition means strong teams, and once a boy is selected, he must cooperate with his teammates. He may be able to run and kick and pass, but if he will not cooperate, he is useless. Teamwork is important.

Competition is a phase of life. Chances for happy marriages are better when boys and girls have large fields for competitive selection. It is not always wise to take the first one that comes along.

In our competitive society, the government is the referee for business. Under the original rules, the government could not be a competitor—but this has gone by the boards as government has gotten into the game.

The duty of the government is to establish justice—fair rules for playing the game with the maximum of freedom. Interference by the government with prices arrived at by buyers and sellers is inequitable. Government interference with the free market is self-defeating, as we shall see.

A new element of competition has appeared in business in the form of "wholesale outlets," "discount houses," or "clubs." Anyone can become a member by entering the front door and signing his name. He pays highly competitive prices, not arbitrary "Fair Trade" prices. The United States Chamber of Commerce recently reported that such establishments carry on 18% of the nation's retail business. (This is not to say, however, that no competition exists among "Fair Trade" prices.)

We live in a competitive world. This country's trade preeminence has been based on freedom of the merchant to sell as he pleases and of the consumer to buy as he pleases. Government fixing of prices brings chaos and legal evasions.

Most new toll roads grant monopolies to one oil concern and one restaurant chain. Prices are noncompetitive and therefore high. Thrifty drivers over the Connecticut, New York, and New Jersey speedways, to avoid these prices, fill tanks and stomachs in the gaps between the restricted highways. State liquor monopolies and cigarette, whiskey, and special taxes bring about exorbitant impositions, often evaded.

Sales-tax states, in defiance of interstate-commerce laws, pressure mail-order houses into collecting the tax on goods shipped to consumers in other states. Some states follow Michigan's example with a "use" tax which compels a resident to pay, if he is caught evading it, an equivalent of the sales tax for anything brought into the state. If he brings it by car, the vehicle may also be confiscated as a penalty. Consumers evade the taxes by ordering from smaller firms that are not so closely watched. Trickery is encouraged.

Labor organizations tend to destroy healthy competition among workers when they increase their demands for government support of the closed shop. The competitive advantage of states having "right to work" laws are confirmed by reports of the United States Census Bureau and of the Department of Labor, which show an employment and population growth in the states where statutory or constitutional protection is provided for the fundamental right of individuals to work without paying tribute to a private organization.

Just as workers compete for jobs, so employers compete for the best employees. They have found that salary is not the only means of attracting workers. Good working conditions are an important consideration. Those employers who can with frankness and fairness, soothe human sensibilities, excite enthusiasm and foster ambition. They therefore benefit from the resulting high morale. Competition, then, can make a job more dignified and pleasant, furnishing powerful incentives for an employee to do his best and constantly improve his abilities.

What is true of employees is true of their employers. An unknown Babbitt has said:

> My competitors do more for me than my friends do. My friends are too polite to point out my weaknesses, but my competitors go to great expense to tell of them.
>
> My competitors are efficient, diligent, and attentive—they make me search for ways to improve my products and my services.
>
> My competitors would take my business away from me if they could. This keeps me alert to keep what I have.
>
> If I had no competitors I would be lazy, incompetent, inattentive. I need the discipline they enforce upon me.
>
> I salute my competitors—they have been good to me. God bless them all.
>
> Healthy personalities enjoy this competitive world. They detest the thought of a humdrum, planned existence.

Chapter Four
INCENTIVE VS. COMPULSION

A RECENT survey of 30,000 high school students showed that 60% believed that profit incentive should be eliminated from our economic system. Like many terms whose basic meaning is perverted by Communist and other propaganda, "profit motive" has come to be a derogatory label attached to the competitive system of free enterprise.

Profits are an important incentive in a free economy; profits and losses function to control and expand the free-enterprise system. They are a day-by-day guide to the working of productive competition.

The competitive and collective systems are no longer mere theories; they have been in operation long enough for a fair judgment of their merits to be formed. The competitive system has made the United States the greatest nation in history, with more comforts, conveniences, and opportunities for happiness than any people have ever enjoyed. The collective system, now enforced for close to half a century in the Soviet Union, barely allows the people the necessities of life. It has achieved important advances in science—as other dictatorships such as Hitler's have done—but at the cost of denying freedom, prosperity, the consolations of religion, free expression, material goods, and personal enterprise to more than 180,000,000 people.

There are two ways, and only two, of making an economic system work. They are incentive, with hope of profit, and compulsion backed by physical force. In a system where there is no reward related to exertion, the only alternative is compulsion. Fear replaces hope, sullen resentment replaces cheerful anticipation, and joyful accomplishment becomes a drudgery. Socialists and Communists say a free economy is actuated by greed. On the contrary, any business man, large or small, can assure you that the quickest way to go bankrupt in a competitive business is to become a little greedy. He cannot even get complacent. In a free-enterprise market, when the profits of an industry are above average, capital is usually plowed back into it until profits become average again or even less. If the industry becomes overextended, low profits or losses become the rule until demand is adjusted to supply.

All persons connected with the industry—working in it or supplying it—benefit materially from its prosperity; to that extent, men's natural desire for rewards is satisfied. But the profit-and-loss machinery is not keyed merely to personal benefit; it is an indication of success or failure of the industry and a tool for developing further its usefulness to the community. It has a social rule, touching the well-being of all the people.

Good will, a reputation for giving reliable goods and services for the money, is generally the best asset a competing concern can have. The competitive system wants to keep its customers alive, satisfied, and coming back with more orders. The collective system, itself both consumer and producer, rations a mere life-sustaining pittance to its customers and executes or starves those who slow down on its labor treadmill.

We work to give our families good homes, good clothes, and opportunities in life. We like to build fine churches, schools, parks, and playgrounds. We create new industries, solve age-old problems, and build beautiful things. Competition gives material rewards to the individual, but a further compensation sought by most persons is the satisfaction of a job well done, the pride of accomplishment, and public recognition.

Orville Wright once said:

When we were carrying on wind-tunnel work, we had no thought of ever trying to build a power airplane. We did that work just for the fun we got out of learning new truths.

We were not thinking of any practical uses at all. We just wanted to show that it was possible to fly. Even for some time afterwards we didn't suppose it would ever be possible to fly or make landings at night.[1]

---

1 Orville Wright quoted by Fred C. Kelly (ed.), *Miracle at Kitty Hawk* (Farrar, Straus & Young, New York, 1951), pp. 416-7.

Incentive is not money alone; joy of accomplishment means much. If you set Americans to digging holes and filling them up again, they will quit in disgust. They want results, individual productiveness, not treadmill conformity. Personal prestige, the admiration and respect of our fellowmen are important. Henry Ford acquired a great fortune, yet it was a small fraction of the value of the benefits he created in employment, profit, and enjoyment for millions of people.

The vital spark of free-enterprise economy is incentive, yet for many years our government has tended to quench it. By subsidizing housing, it discourages private housing. It retards private investment in manufacturing plants by subsidizing a few competitors in industry. It owns 25 percent of the power systems in the country, in tax-free competition with tax-paying companies that are required to help support, with taxes, unfair government competition. Price ceilings, wage limits, confiscatory taxes, allocation of materials all stifle incentive.

James Cash Penney, born in 1875, visited Washington in 1954 to christen his 1,650th store. His first clerking job, in 1895, paid $2.27 a *month*. Four years later, a $50 offer attracted him to Wyoming. In another 12 years he had $2,000, three-fourths of it borrowed, to buy in with two partners who owned six country stores selling everything from yeast cakes to a roll of barbed wire. Six stores grew to twenty-five, and these to fifty, and now Penney stores are in every state. Individual initiative and profit sharing with employees created these stores, in striking contrast to the lack of incentive in a government-planned economy. Mr. Penney said:

> Every time we open a new store, everybody profits, competitors as well as customers. Free competition is not a dog-eat-dog struggle for a limited amount of business. It is a healthy spur to each merchant, better service for the public, and more business in the area.[2]

Mr. Penney has built institutions with endowments in millions for undenominational religion, worthy old persons, and for improving Guernsey cattle.

---

2 J. C. Penney, "Competition" (The J. C. Penney Co., New York), p. 1.

Giant companies such as Sears Roebuck, Montgomery Ward, Spiegel and Alden, with a combined sales of $4,250,000,000, help to make Chicago the center of the country's far-reaching mail-order business. The first venture was launched by A. Montgomery Ward and his brother-in-law, George R. Thorne, in 1872 with a total capital of $2,400. The company got its start as supply house for the Grangers, a farm organization fighting Eastern monopoly prices for farm equipment at that early date. The company now does an annual business of close to $2,000,000.

In 1886, Richard W. Sears was a twenty-year-old station agent at North Redwood, Minnesota. A local jeweler who had too many watches refused a shipment. Sears asked the Elgin factory to let him try selling them instead of paying charges for their return. Other agents bought, and he opened an office in Minneapolis, later moving to Chicago, to sell by mail to the public. Alvah C. Roebuck, an Indiana farm boy, answered an advertisement for a watchmaker, and the world's largest merchandising organization was started. Julius Rosenwald, a clothier on Chicago's West Side, bought into the partnership in 1895. Five years later, annual sales had grown from $800,000 to $11,000,000.

Retired General Robert E. Wood became manager. Realizing that, with the automobile, shopping areas were no longer limited by walking distance, he started retail stores in city suburbs. The company now has some 750 stores in this country and Latin America and a dozen mail-order plants in addition to the immense one in Chicago. Annual sales are around $3,000,000,000. Its seven catalogs a year, of which 50,000,000 are printed, list 100,000 items at prices from five cents to $1,500. Assets of its employees' profit-sharing, savings and retirement funds are in eight figures.

"No regimented economy can hope to compete in dynamic drive with an economy which possesses nearly ten million independent centers of initiative,"[3] Professor Sumner H. Slichter of Harvard University once declared. This statement strikes with force today as we compare privately owned stores in the United States with government-owned stores in the Soviet Union. The contrast between free competition and controlled col-

---

3 Sumner H. Slichter, Letter to Joel R. Belknap dated December 1953.

lectivism is tremendous. And the contrast is not between theories alone but between two actual sets of conditions.

Izvestia, the Soviet government newspaper, recently told of the plight of stores in that country. The manager of the state's largest department store—GUM, in Moscow—tells his troubles, unbelievable to an American merchant or customer. His store, glorified before the world in Communist propaganda, has cloth for suits and dresses, he says, but its notions department has no trimmings. It is short of electrical fixtures and kitchen utensils, even simple baking tins. It has bicycles, phonographs, radios, and refrigerators but no replacement parts. These expensive articles, for which an ordinary worker must skimp for a year, are not guaranteed. If one of them breaks down, it cannot be repaired; government factories will not supply spare parts or even answer orders from the big store. Spare parts do not show on a factory's production quota, and statistics are the test of Soviet production. The same applies to children's booties. The manager ordered 200,000 pairs and got 22,000.

The manager tells sadly of six months' effort to get broomsticks for "make-it-yourself" customers. After several weeks had passed without a reply from the People's Woodenware Trust, he decided the Trust was not going to fill his order. His purchasing agents traveled to several factories without success. He finally took his order to the chairman of the Central Council of the Soviet Union in Moscow, where the top planners officiate. The chairman sent it, with proper endorsement, to the Central Council of the Russian Republic. It moved through channels to the Provincial Council and several others before reaching the Woodenware Trust. This time a reply came back slowly through the same channels. The manager was informed that no timber could be spared for broomsticks, and, what was more conclusive, there was no machinery for making a broomstick. If the proletariat want broomsticks, they can whittle them out as their forefathers did.

Before the Communists consolidated their police power, Lenin saved the faltering national economy once by permitting "NEP," the New Economic Policy. Private business was again sanctioned in violation of the Communist dogma of government ownership. A revolution was prevented, but as the police grew stronger the new ventures were nationalized and the drab government monopoly has since become complete.

THE STORY OF FREE ENTERPRISE

Clarence Manion, former dean of the Notre Dame Law School, says of big government:

> If big and all-powerful government was the secret of general popular welfare, Europe would have been the land of milk and honey, while the history of the United States would be a story of misery, poverty, and destitution. The facts are the other way round. Europe's record proves that big and all-powerful government, whether its sanction be royal, democratic or revolutionary, produces general *warfare* instead of general *welfare* and promotes penury and pestilence rather than progress and prosperity.[4]

When Karl Marx put into practical operation the basic idea of communism—"From each according to his abilities, to each according to his needs"[5]—he found that the slowest and most incompetent workers set the pace.

The severest punishments—food-ration cuts, prison sentences, and executions—could raise production little above the starvation level. And an enormous police force was required.

Experiment proved that, even under the Soviet system, a degree of incentive would bring results.

Russian factory workers now are on piecework, with bonuses for betterment of quantity and quality. They have the "Stakhanov Watch," a period of a week or more in which extra-skilled workers or efficiency experts take over a factory. Special incentives are offered such as prizes and vacations. A good worker may even get to ride in an automobile and be cheered by the crowds. Factory "norms" are often exceeded, but when the adulated worker returns to his job he finds a new "norm" which may be twice as high as the old one.

---

4 Clarence Manion, *The Key to Peace* (Heritage Foundation, Inc., Chicago, 1951), p. 55.
5 Karl Marx, "Critique of the Gotha Programme" (May, 1875), *Marx and Engels Selected Works* (Foreign Languages Publishing House, Moscow, 1955), Vol. II, pp. 23-4.

JOEL R. BELKNAP

A modest but typical demonstration of the superiority of American incentive and cooperation over compulsion and violence was given in Toledo, Ohio. The Mather Spring Company started to supply big automobile builders in 1911. In 1952, it realized that competition could be met only by modernizing equipment and methods and increasing man-hour production. An outside concern made a study and reported its findings to executives and to the union. The union, rather than deciding that the troubles were not its headache, cooperated; it consented to job regrading and some temporary layoffs and agreed that "we will go places together." The company reported that in two years costs were reduced, the product improved, employment and sales doubled, job security assured, and only one written union grievance had been submitted in that time.

Under a system of incentive management developed during the late 1940's by James F. Lincoln, of the Lincoln Electric Company, Cleveland, Lincoln employees produced annually an average per man of more than $25,000 of electrical equipment. This is about twice the average output of a worker in all other manufacturing industries and is two and a half times the output in the electrical-machine-manufacturing industry. Lincoln employees earned the highest individual pay, but the labor cost of the company's products for a dollar of sales was the lowest among all comparable industries. Mr. Lincoln said:

> Money incentive for more production is not itself necessarily the means that will get increased production. Money alone will not give the American worker the incentive that he wants and eventually must get if industrial progress is to continue and the American way of life is to survive and constantly grow better.[6]

"Recognition of our abilities by our contemporaries and by ourselves" is the key to Mr. Lincoln's system. That means, of course, making an ample profit; while people do not strive only for a big bank account, they do

---

6 James F. Lincoln, Letter to Mary Borden McManus dated August 20, 1962.

strive for the things money can bring: nice homes, fine cars, education for the children, high places in the esteem of their fellow men.

Incentive management is not easy. The difficulties are great. But the Lincoln system makes obsolete the old class warfare of labor versus management and it holds great promise for the future.

Many substitutes for financial incentives exist. In Europe there are titles, and the heads of a great corporation often are made lords or knights. Social distinction, honors, ribbons, and uniforms appeal to many people. George S. Benson of Harding College points out:

> As the strength of a rope is the sum of the strength of its individual fibers, that nation will be strongest which provides the best incentives for every individual to do his best.
>
> Freedom for each individual to retain the fruit of his industry is the incentive for this country's unparalleled progress. The economic weakness and stagnation of European countries are due to the fact that they have largely destroyed incentives. They have failed to use the great power of justified self-interest. It is the hope of profits, together with the fear of loss risked with every investment, that makes the American system function and function well. [7]

An industrialist, Crawford H. Greenewalt, president of the du Pont Company, puts the same idea differently:

> Much has been said of the vulgarity of the money motive, but I doubt one could find a cleaner and more honest basis for rewarding high performance. A desire for power is surely less worthy, and I cannot believe that efforts to win the admiration of the crowds are ethically more desirable.[8]

---

[7] George S. Benson, Letter to Mary Borden McManus dated August 20, 1962.
[8] Crawford H. Greenwalt, "What Kind of Incentives?" Speech before Annual Dinner, Illinois State Chamber of Commerce, Chicago, October 19, 1951, p. 6.

JOEL R. BELKNAP

To the majority of Americans, competitive business is a fascinating game. Many men past retirement age who have plenty on which to live out their lives in idleness do not retire, because they enjoy their accomplishments. This passion for usefulness is something the Communists cannot understand. They label it "greed."

Chapter Five
FREE ENTERPRISE, CAPITALISM, CONSUMERISM

In a Free market, men are encouraged to increase their output so that they will have more goods and services to exchange for things they want. Their income depends on their production, at fair prices, of things that others want.

Men are rewarded in accordance with their contributions to the economy.

It rarely happens that anyone benefits unfairly at another's expense in such a market. When unfair benefits appear, look for government intervention in favor of some pressure group.

The essence of the free market is individual freedom. The free market is the most democratic institution on earth. It is a vast auction, where a jury of millions of consumers passes daily judgment on the goods and services offered.

It is the fairest market ever devised, for seller, buyer, and public. It is the main source of economic justice and, while imperfect, it is the best means of assuring the people a fair relationship between the price of what they produce and the price of the goods and services they buy.

Intervention

The rigging or crippling of this free market by the government is morally wrong. Interference with its orderly working may be justified by a national emergency, but continued interference as a political principle leads to the plundering of one class of citizens for the profit of others.

When political control of prices is substituted for the free market, costs are increased for some, and everybody pays higher taxes, including those receiving the largess. General welfare becomes secondary to getting more votes in the bag.

Government defiance of the free market for farm products is steadily approaching a national catastrophe. It ignores the economic law of supply and demand and is a waste, a great expense, and a discrimination against the American people. The government is now swamped with many billions of dollars' worth of food.

Instead of selling this surplus at cost to the American people, who have paid for it in taxes, the government either lets it rot in storage or tries to force it on foreign countries as a gift or at less than cost. This complicates our relations with other nations who are producing the same food and are seeking world markets for it.

The crop-support program is pictured as giving the farmer the same relative income and purchasing power as other citizens. Actually, it demoralizes agriculture and the entire national economy by raising the costs of farm production and therefore the prices of all commodities. The program guarantees the sale of basic farm crops and fixes a minimum price level. Certain grains, dairy products, and many other crops are specified. If a farmer cannot sell these in the free market, the government will buy them at a "parity price."

When the program started, parity was figured by comparing the prices a farmer received with those he paid for specified necessities of family or farm during the base period of 1910 to 1914. As his costs increased each year, the parity price for farm products would increase proportionately. Truck farms were not in the program, and labor was not included in farm costs.

The base index years for figuring prices have moved forward as the dollar has depreciated. Parity prices are the same for the entire country, although costs vary widely in different areas. The reappraising and changing of items in the index has not kept pace, and never can keep pace, with progress. Farmers use more fertilizer and insecticides, machinery has reduced man-hours but not labor costs.

The great potato fiasco of 1949 was the direct result of the crop-support program. A high price swamped the government with potatoes.

Farmers bought them back for hog feed at less than the cost of the sacks. Poison was poured over mountains of potatoes, and guards were hired to prevent people from getting other potatoes for food before they rotted.

The desk-tied farmers in Washington then reversed the controls and set a maximum price for potatoes. It was so low that farmers stopped raising them for sale to the government, and another black market was born. Penalties for going above the fixed price were severe.

Many farmers are fully aware of the fallacies of subsidies and controls. Writes Judge William G. Davison of Oklahoma, representative of a cattleman's association:

> Most cattlemen of my acquaintance do not want either subsidies or price supports. When producers accept government handouts, they must take government regulations and controls along with them. When this happens, we are driving headlong toward national socialism and the destruction of our free enterprise system. That we are not prepared to accept.[1]

Stabilization of markets and values is the avowed purpose of control, but the results are disappointing, as shown by the violent production swings of commodities under monopolistic control by government agencies.

Winthrop W. Aldrich, financier and diplomat, points out the fallacy of government intervention in these words:

> Our price system is made of different kinds of prices, wages, rents, stock market quotations, interest rates, charges for professional services and many others. All of these prices are continually fluctuating in response to underlying conditions of supply and demand and in so doing they direct every phase of economic activity. The free price mechanism is probably the only possible device which can weld the personal and individually determined preferences, desires and ambitions of men into a social order.

---

1 William G. Davisson, Article opposing price supports or price control for livestock, Tulsa *World*, December 6, 1953.

JOEL R. BELKNAP

> Under a regime of governmentally fixed prices the continuance of democratic institutions is impossible. A government undertaking delicate price dictation can tolerate no criticism. [2]

In a free market, prices, not political patronage or votes, control the production, marketing, and consumption of goods and services. The interplay of prices automatically brings production and consumption into balance. An increase in demand for a product raises its price and immediately stimulates production. A decrease in demand lowers the price and decreases production. When there is a large crop of wheat and a short crop of corn, poultry feed will contain a larger portion of wheat and a lower cracked-corn content. The free market, impersonal, flexible, and automatic, makes thousands of such adjustments everyday and everywhere. It rewards efficient producers because greater quantities are demanded from those whose costs are lowest.

Government supports and price ceilings create class distinctions and set one section of the population against others. Government intervention arouses suspicion and resentment whenever the people become informed. With some $10,000,000,000 sunk in farm surpluses, our government is buying still more. Storage alone costs over $365,000,000 a year. More than 2,000,000,000 bushels of corn and 1,000,000,000 of wheat fill every grain elevator, four hundred idle ships, village streets, boxes, and bins. Some grain is ten years old and too deteriorated for flour or even livestock food. Butter, peanuts, turkeys, cotton, and other crops add to the useless hoards.

The government announces acreage quotas while spending billions for irrigation so that the farmer can increase crops by closer planting and the use of more fertilizer. An Indiana farm increased its corn crop this way from 42 to 127 bushels an acre without violating the quota.

In 1956 the Soil Bank scheme was enacted into law, with its many provisions and penalties. It simply pays subsidies to farmers to let certain lands lie fallow; the farmers may not farm them nor even graze cattle on them.

---

2 Winthrop W. Aldrich quoted in letter from John S. Ames, Jr. to Joel R. Belknap, December 1, 1953.

A "crop-cop" of the United States Department of Agriculture once explained the law to a group of Indiana farmers, saying, "We are going to bend over backwards on this thing. If I am driving along the road and I see that some of your cows have broken through a fence and are pasturing on restricted soil bank land, I'll stop and even help you get the cows back where they belong. I might even do it a second time. But if it happened again, I am afraid I would have to assume it was no coincidence and get tough."

The Welfare State is a Police State.

"The Man with the Hoe"

Through centuries of recorded history in many other nations, the plight of the man with the hoe—the peasant—has remained as the poet Edwin Markham described it:

> Bowed by the weight of centuries he leans
> Upon his hoe and gazes on the ground,
> The emptiness of ages in his face,
> And on his back the burden of the world.
> Who made him dead to rapture and despair,
> A thing that grieves not and that never hopes,
> Stolid and stunned, a brother to the ox?[3]

When this republic was founded, the man with the hoe was set free. He was recognized as having certain unalienable rights, the greatest of which was economic liberty—freedom from molestation. The American peasant became a farmer, and farming a technical profession.

With his capital goods limited to a hoe, worth perhaps a dollar, he could cultivate three acres of ground by working from daylight to dark. He worked hard—and produced a little more than he consumed. Here he was able to add a mule, a plow, and a harrow to his capital goods, and he could cultivate twenty or thirty acres. He then produced more

---

3 *The Home Book of Verse* (Henry Holt & Co., New York, 1953), p.3041.

and acquired a team of horses, a few cows, better ploughs, seeders, and harvesters. He sent a son to an agricultural school, and when the boy returned, the farmer got a tractor and cultivated still more ground. He learned about fertilizers, better plants and soil conservation.

Investment in education is also a capital asset.

This story, duplicated by thousands of American families, shows why a single farmer can now feed twice as many as he did forty years ago. *It points up the importance of surplus, of profit, the vital necessity of producing more than the producer himself consumes in order to accumulate capital goods.* Abraham Lincoln said:

> The prudent, penniless beginner labors for wages for a while, saves a surplus with which to buy tools or land for himself; . . . and at length hires another beginner to help him. This is the just and generous, and prosperous system, which opens the way to all—gives hope to all, and consequently energy and progress, and improvement of conditions to all.[4]

The standard of living of the American man with the hoe and his descendants grew with his capital investment. *His emancipation came with the increase of his capital store of technical and mechanical power.* This is how free enterprise operates.

For each of the 8.5 million farm operators, hired hands, and family workers on farms today, there is an average capital investment of more than $15,000.

Capitalism

The *Standard Home Reference Dictionary* defines capitalism as "a system that favors the concentration of capital in the hands of a few." Then it

---

[4] Abraham Lincoln, "Annual Message to Congress," December 1, 1862, quoted by Roy P. Basler (ed.), *The Collected Works of Abraham Lincoln* (Rutgers University Press, New Brunswick, New Jersey, 1953), Vol. V., p. 537.

THE STORY OF FREE ENTERPRISE

defines "capital" as "wealth employed in or available for production" and "any resource or circumstance that can be utilized for an ambitious or self-interested object."

This definition of capitalism seems to be in accord with the ideas of Karl Marx. In 1883 Marx "foresaw" that capitalism would foster great monopolies and cartels owned by fewer and fewer persons, finally and inevitably to be superseded by communism.

The Socialists charge that "unearned income"—rents, royalties, and dividends—is concentrated in the hands of a few. The fact is that in 1944 those earning less than $5,000 a year received 69.4% of all rents and 69.4% of all interest and dividends, according to the Bureau of Economic Research of Notre Dame University.

In 1944, 90% of all salaries and wages went to persons earning less than $5,000 a year.

More recent estimates indicate that over fifteen million shareholders have a stake in our economy, and their number is rapidly growing. Housewives are the largest single group of investors—34%. Union pension funds are well into the billions of dollars. Over half of the eighty billion dollars' worth of railroads and utilities is owned by persons who earn less than $7,500 annually, and this group owns two thirds of the wealth. Many large concerns have far more stockholders than employees. Thousands of indirect stockholders own shares of mutual funds.

If you have a few dollars in a bank, or insurance, or a few savings bonds or stocks, you are to that extent a capitalist. Those who finish high school earn on the average $3,600 a year, while those who complete college average at least $6,000 a year. Is not education a form of capital?

It is widely assumed that the American economic system is entirely owned and controlled by "big business," in monopolistic fashion. What is "big business"? The following are some concerns usually held to constitute "big business":

American Tel. & Tel. Co.
Standard Oil Co. of N.J.
Socony Vacuum Oil Co.

General Motors Corp.
Chrysler Corp.
U.S. Steel Corp.
Bethlehem Steel Corp.
E. I. du Pont de Nemours.
Pacific Gas & Electric Co.
Consolidated Ed. Co. of N.Y.
Anaconda Copper Mining Co.
Kennecott Copper Corp.
Bank of America (Calif.)
National City Bank of N.Y.
American Tobacco Co.
R. J. Reynolds Tobacco Co.
Union Carbide & Carbon.
Pennsylvania R.R. Co.
Santa Fe R.R. Co.
General Electric Co.
Westinghouse Electric Co.
Sears, Roebuck & Co.
Montgomery Ward & Co.
Ford Motor Co.
Swift & Co.
General Foods Corp.
Goodyear Tire & Rubber Co.
Firestone Tire & Rubber Co.
The Great A. & P. Co.
Safeway Stores, Inc.
Proctor & Gamble.

The total assets of these corporations (omitting the Ford Motor Co.) in 1954 were $56 billions. Our "big government" in one year spends more than the total assets of "big business." Consumers' personal income is $300 billions annually. "Big business," therefore, accounts for a small fraction of all business.

Consumerism

Mr. and Mrs. Consumer are the bosses of our economic system. They employ the employers. They determine what shall be produced, how much, when, and at what price. John S. Bugas of the Ford Motor Company once suggested that the term "consumerism," is a more fitting term, perhaps, than "capitalism."

As consumers we constitute a great classless society. As producers we may work forty hours a week for a paycheck, but the instant we spend a cent of it we join the consumers, and our interest as consumers is exactly as great as our concern as producers. What dollars will buy for the consumer is just as important as the number of dollars in the consumer's paycheck.

Free-enterprise "consumerism" is the only system that belongs to *all* the people as consumers. It is a democratic institution if there ever was one. The cash register is a voting machine. Every penny spent is a vote that is counted and studied by experts with accounting machines.

Free enterprise is not the sole property of the great corporations, and no one knows that better than the heads of the corporations themselves. Benjamin F. Fairless, when he was president of the United States Steel Corporation, said:

> Free Enterprise is the only system on this earth which richly profits all the people; for it is also the only system on this earth which truly belongs to all the people. It is not the private possession of American business, nor of any other economic group—and it never can be. It is the property—and the responsibility—of every man and woman in this nation.[5]

And Crawford H. Greenewalt, as head of the du Pont Company:

---

5 Benjamin F. Fairless, *Who Profits from Free Enterprise?* Talk before the Manufacturers' Association of Connecticut, Inc., Yale University, New Haven, September 21, 1954 (United States Steel Corp., New York, 1954), p. 18.

> The only power corporations have, whether they be large or small, is the right to stand in the market place and cry their wares. If the customers find those wares good, they will buy and the corporations will prosper. If they do not, the proprietor will soon be sitting on the curbstone, whether we are talking about a large manufacturer or a roadside market.[6]

In a perfectly free economy, those who serve society best accumulate large resources, as the Ford Motor Company and many others have done. Now, with our steeply graduated tax system—perfectly in accord with Karl Marx's ideas—capital accumulation takes place much more slowly. Had our present tax rates prevailed forty years ago, such concerns as Ford and General Motors could not be half as productive as they are.

Management and Labor

The stockholders of a corporation are franchised according to the number of shares each holds. They elect the board of directors. The directors then select the president and other executive officers. Stockholders, sometimes a few, sometimes numbering hundreds of thousands, are responsible for management; their votes are necessary for approval or disapproval of top policy decisions.

Stockholders strive to invest money in organizations whose services are in greatest demand by the public. They withdraw their capital from failing businesses. They interpret the orders of their bosses, the consumers, and their success or failure as owners depends upon the correctness of their interpretations.

We all are employers. We work forty hours a week for a paycheck. We may average eight hours of sleep a day, or fifty-six hours a week. That gives ninety-six hours for working and sleeping—with travel time, say one

---

[6] Crawford H. Greenwalt, Statement before the Special Sub-Committee on Study of Monopoly Power of the Committee on the Judiciary, House of Representatives, November 15, 1949.

hundred hours a week. With 168 hours in a week, we have about sixty-eight hours to enjoy the benefits of our paychecks. We may employ the local groceryman or a giant chain to supply us with food. Every payment on our automobile reimburses the finance company a little for meeting the salaries and wages of the automobile manufacturer from the president down.

A full-page advertisement of one of the new models is the bid of an automobile manufacturer for the job of building cars for you and me. The company may speculate a little and build a stock of cars ahead, on the chance that we will buy them. That does not alter the fact that you and thousands of others must give jobs to that automobile company or it will shut down.

Labor Unions

Many believe that the high wages and high purchasing power of an hour of labor are due entirely to labor unions. Yet England has been highly unionized for many years and has made little progress in raising the living standard of her working people. Italy and France are also unionized, but the unions alone have done very little toward raising the standards of living of their members.

The sustaining theory of unionism is that it provides "collective bargaining." A trade union should be a cooperative development where the employees are on an equal bargaining basis with their employer. It is necessary that there be no monopoly control either by the powerful employer against weak unions, or the powerful unions against weak employers. The individual workman must be protected against both.

Organized labor can increase real wages only when a part—not all—of the people are organized. Suppose everyone, white-collar workers, landlords, bankers, small and big businessmen, and investors, were to organize and attain monopoly power, then manage to double their incomes. This would have exactly the same result as simply doubling prices by increasing the money supply.

Under twenty years of government favorable to them, unions have become powerful in this country. They are organized on an industry-wide basis. One man can shut down the coal mines. Another can stop all truck transport. A few can shut down nearly all the steel mills. A few more can stop the railroads. Others can stop all shipping at the Atlantic, Pacific, and Gulf ports.

No employer or group of employers is powerful enough to deal with such large organizations, which in some cases do not hesitate to call strikes—in the coal mines, for example—in the middle of a war for survival of the nation. So the unions often find themselves face to face with the government. The government "took over" the coal mines and the railroads and endeavored to take over the steel mills.

The unions had disregarded the advice of Samuel Gompers, who headed the American Federation of Labor in its most difficult period, to "stay out of politics." He said that he would cast his vote that the men of labor should not willingly enslave themselves to governmental authority in their industrial effort for freedom. William Green, who succeeded Mr. Gompers, said that labor and capitol have a common cause in protecting themselves against governmental agencies usurping power over them.

When the government seized the steel mills in 1952, a congressman declared:

> This substitutes the whim of the politicians for the rule of law. If a president can raise wages in a key industry by fiat, he can lower them as arbitrarily. If he can decree the closed shop, he can also destroy trade unionism.

Political influence has resulted in wage increases by government order. This is one phase of price fixing, and is destructive to the free market and the free economy.

A government that undertakes wage and price dictation cannot tolerate criticism—it degenerates into a tyranny.

No dictator has ever restored freedom of opportunity and freedom of occupational movement.

John V. Van Sickle of the Indiana Chamber of Commerce has said:

> The really dangerous threat of monopoly in this country arises when management and a union get together and agree to restrict entry of capital and labor into a field, thus to create artificial scarcity and exploit customers. The possibility of this happening increases as the jurisdiction of the union expands. Once a union gains control of an entire industry it virtually forces all of the plants in the industry to get together and work out a common policy. A cartel is in formation. The real threat of monopoly today comes from the side of labor.[7]

Is this situation not a standing invitation for a dictator to take over?

Wages of employes, plant maintenance, owners' profits, and other expenses naturally come from the "added value," the amount a factory adds by converting raw material into a marketable article. The proportion of added value varies according to the industry. In a furniture factory, lumber is cheap, but in an automobile plant most of the material is already fabricated and expensive. Contrary to widely accepted ideas, however, the division of the added value among material, labor, and profits remains fairly constant in each line of industry. Increased costs cannot be absorbed by reducing wages and profits without wrecking the company. Consequently, the only way to avoid spiraling prices and to continue competition is to increase production and sales and reduce costs.

The government's Statistical Abstract gives many figures on this complex subject. It shows a century of change in American industry in the use of manpower, animal power, and steam, gas, oil, and water power:

---

[7] John W. Van Sickle, *Union Wage Policy and Employment*, Talk before Indiana State Chamber of Commerce, February 26, 1948 (Indiana State Chamber of Commerce, Indianapolis, 1948), p. 7.

Year	Man	Animal	Artificial
1850	20%	50%	30%
1900	15%	30%	55%
1950	6%	—	94%

Another table shows the percentage of union workers in factories and their only slightly changed percentage of the added value in spite of all the wage increases over nearly forty years:

Year	Union Workers	Added Value to Workers
1909	9%	39.2%
1923	11%	41.3%
1947	65%	40.7%

When the automobile industry was unorganized, between 1929 and 1933, worker's wages were 13.8 cents of each dollar of gross sales. In 1937, after successful strikes and almost complete unionization, labor's share rose to 14.6 cents. In the steel industry, from 1929 to 1932, before organization, labor received 20 cents of each sales dollar. In 1939, completely unionized, labor's share had declined to 19.9 cents. It seems that the only way for labor to obtain increases in real wages is to cooperate with management for increased production—to produce larger shares for all. When wages are arbitrarily raised, the incomes of others are made lower. Your income is my outgo.

Richard Gray of the Building and Construction Trades Union said:

> ... unless top labor and top management form some basis for reaching an understanding, we can expect more and more participation by the Federal Government into the activities of private enterprise. Contrary to the thinking of many people, it is my belief that the majority of labor does not look with favor upon the Federal Government usurping the functions of private enterprise.[8]

---

[8] Richard Gray, quoted in *Building and Construction Trades Bulletin*, February, 1952, p. 2.

THE STORY OF FREE ENTERPRISE

Professor E. Wight Bakke of Yale writes:

> Collective bargaining *can* be made the democratic instrument for securing industrial peace and stability. It must be made so. Otherwise the struggle will be shunted off into the field of politics. If this happens, men will influence the management of industry directly, face to face, in the places where they work and on issues with which they are familiar. They will influence management by the roundabout method of bringing influence to bear on government. That is the beginning of the end, if not the end itself, of free enterprise *and* free unions.[9]

Left-wing labor papers continue to advocate government ownership of industries. But government ownership of industries deprives workers of the right to strike. President Truman's orders for government seizure of the steel mills forbade interference in their operation by workers; in other words, "No strikes!"

In 1951 the government issued a paper covering its "general policy relative to organized employees." It was endorsed by the Federal Personnel Council and had the general approval of the Civil Service Commission and the White House. It established an open shop and a no-strike policy for federal employees.

Under socialism the right to strike becomes sabotage. The Socialist Labor Government of England used the army to break strikes on nearly 500 occasions. As all industry in the Soviet Union is owned by the Government, strikes are punished as treason. One of the first acts of the Chinese Communist Government was a decree providing:

> Employees shall not strike, or engage in other activities tending to obstruct production or to produce deterioration in labor discipline. Even after an arbitrary decision has been made by the bureau [of social

---

9 E. Wight Bakke, "Obstacles to Labor-Management Survival, *The Reader's Digest*, November, 1952, p. 69.

affairs] the right of interpretation and revision of these regulations rests with the military control commission.[10]

The exiled anti-Communist Chinese labor leader, Lu Chiang-Shih, announced over the Formosa radio that the Communists had murdered a thousand former Chinese labor leaders and that ten times that number were slowly dying in jail.

Union Discipline

Managers of industrial concerns prefer to deal with a labor union rather than with non-union workers, because they get much better worker discipline. When a manager thinks workers are loafing or doing inferior work, he says nothing to the workers but notifies a union official. The union official can talk to the workers in a manner which, if it came from management, would cause an immediate strike.

The handling of "wildcat" strikes is left to union officials.

To be fired by a company may not be a serious matter, but to be thrown out of an industry-wide union may deprive a worker of his only means of livelihood.

Automation

Now, there is much discussion about automation—automatic or "push-button" factories—which many fear will cause unemployment. But the only thing new about the principle of automation seems to be the name.

In 1847, Oliver Evans built a flour mill near Philadelphia that was completely automatic. We have mentioned the ship assembly line of the Arsenal at Venice in the 15th century.

---

10 "Regulations Governing the Procedures for the Settlement of Labor Disputes," Article 6, The State Council, Republic of China, November 16, 1950.

THE STORY OF FREE ENTERPRISE

An automatic loom that wove complicated textile patterns from punched cards antedates by 150 years the business machines of today that are controlled by punched cards and tape (in spite of these, the number of accountants and auditors increased 70% from 1940 to 1950).

When the spinning-jenny and power shuttle loom were introduced into England, unemployment followed. Rioters smashed machinery. But within a few years, with power machinery, ten persons were employed for every one that had worked on the old hand looms, and an hour of labor would buy more clothing than ever before.

A factory president recently said, "We started with twelve men. We have purchased every labor-saving device that came along. Now we employ eight hundred."

The dial telephone displaced thousands of telephone operators between 1940 and 1950, but the number of telephone employees increased by 159,000, or 79%.

The real wages of workers, measured in purchasing power, have advanced at almost exactly the same rate as the improvement in productivity. According to the United States Census of Manufacture, from 1914 to 1947 productivity increased by 161%. It is well within the possible errors in the statistics to say that this is the same as the increase in worker income. Where automation improves production, it should raise real wages.

"Labor saving" is a poor description of machinery. "High production" is better. Because of "high-production" machinery, we have abundance. Countries like China and India, which have little "labor-saving" machinery, have a surplus of unemployed, low wages, and low living standards. In this country, which makes maximum use of modern machinery, labor is scarce and highly paid. But the Communists refuse to learn from our workers' experience.

Big Business Versus Little Business

Karl Marx predicted that big business would devour small industries until only a few monopolies remained. Following his lead, those who favor a planned economy for America have long used big business as a whipping boy. They charge that big business cannot be managed efficiently, that it does not owe its growth to efficiency but to monopoly, and that it retards inventive progress. Then, in contradiction, they argue that big business operates so efficiently that it drives out little businesses.

The fact is that big businesses and little businesses are interdependent. Little businesses are the customers of the giants, and vice-versa. A good example of how they mesh in the nation's economy is found in the report of the Aircraft Industries Association. The thirty-five largest aircraft manufacturing firms are in business in a big way. In one year $2 billion was expended in sub-contracts to some 50,000 small firms scattered throughout the fifty states. An additional $1 billion went to small businesses indirectly because of other dealings. These 50,000 small firms are dependent for some part of their business on the thirty-five biggest firms. But the thirty-five are also dependent on the smaller ones.

An automobile has about 8,000 parts. General Motors buys materials and services from 21,000 other concerns, for which those concerns are paid nearly half of all the money General Motors takes in.

There are virtues in big businesses and small, and the nation's economy is geared to their happy coexistence. Small business is in business in a big way.

The government, however, has tipped the scales in favor of big business by blanket laws and regulations because only the large companies can afford the cost of the lawyers, accountants, and tax experts necessary to conform to the complex laws and regulations.

Big concerns manage to retain undistributed profits for expansion, but controls and taxes for welfare socialism increase the risk for entrepreneurs and permit the small firms to grow slowly if at all.

The federal government now takes 52% of business earnings. In addition, the stockholders pay taxes on dividends, estimated to average another 13 percentage points. Big government has a mathematically greater stake in exploitation of labor and production of profits than does big business.

But how large are the profits of the large business concerns?

A poll was once taken to find the public's estimate of the profits of the meat packers, dry-goods stores, and chain food stores. A majority of

THE STORY OF FREE ENTERPRISE

10,500 people in several large cities were of the opinion that profits averaged 25 cents to 50 cents per dollar of sales. Only 3% of those polled came close to the true figures:

Four-fifths of a cent profit was averaged by meat packers Armour, Swift, and Wilson;

Two cents profit was averaged by dry-goods stores Marshall Field, Gimbels, and Halle Brothers;

Seven-tenths of a cent was averaged by chain food stores Kroger, A.&P., and Safeway.

Chapter Six
PROSPERITY AND DEPRESSIONS

Under the self-regulating features of the free market, supply, signaled by a rise in price, usually increases to meet demand. As supply increases, the price tends to become lower, sometimes lower than before the movement began.

However, one essential thing in our free economy is not self-regulating, and that is its speed.

During the 1952 presidential campaign, much political capital was made by the Democrats of the depression in the 1930's, which began under Republican President Herbert Hoover. By vigorous publicity, the Democrats created the impression that President Hoover and the Republicans were personally responsible for the depression. In 1952 the Democrats confidently predicted that, if a Republican president were elected, another depression would promptly ensue.

Pretending that depressions are synonymous with a political party is typical campaign oratory in an election year. Both parties fear a depression like the plague, but neither party is immune to one. A serious depression occurred in the 1890's during the administration of Grover Cleveland, a Democrat. President Cleveland and his party were severely blamed for that depression, and the Democrats did not elect a president for sixteen years. Depressions are not respecters of political parties. They afflicted the world long before either of our political parties was formed. The more we study depressions the more we are convinced that, while political parties do little to prevent them, they do much to cause them and to make the slumps more severe than otherwise.

Arthur F. Burns, chief economic adviser to former President Eisenhower, once wrote:

The only things we can be reasonably sure of in the proximate future are, first, that our economic system will continue to generate cyclical tendencies, and second, that the government will at some stage intervene to check their course.[1]

Conditions before the crash of October 1929 show little inflation of the dollar. From 1923 to 1929 it remained well stabilized between 82 and 83 cents (1929 basis). But there was much speculation in commodities and the stock market, and the whole story, in brief, was this:

1. Our tariff acts 821 and 822 blighted European trade.
2. Our government, and certain individuals, loaned vast sums to foreign countries in the early 1920's.
3. Those governments used the loans mainly in welfare state projects.
4. Price, rent, and commodity controls caused housing shortages.
5. Labor and material costs of building and industry got far out of line.
6. Governments went heavily into public housing.
7. Much of the money loaned by us abroad came back to speculate in our stock markets. The greatest stock boom in history, based on low margins, followed.
8. The depression was worldwide, precipitated largely by the economic measures of foreign governments. Early in 1929, European bank reserves were permitted to fall from 40 to 21 percent. European currencies depreciated in proportion. To rebuild their gold reserves late in 1929, the countries sold everything that could be converted into gold. They dumped American stocks and bonds on the market, which had been boomed to an all-time peak with the aid of the Dawes loans and American investments abroad. This broke the stock and bond market.
9. Another foreign factor was the silver-market manipulations of Great Britain. Silver reached an all-time high of $1.35 an ounce

---

[1] Arthur F. Burns, *Frontiers of Economic Knowledge* (Princeton University Press, 1954), p. 175.

in 1919. Great Britain withdrew her silver currency, which then was 92½ percent silver, and replaced it with coins containing 50 percent silver. The excess silver was sold on the Shanghai market, causing the price to drop 50 percent in one year. It finally dropped to 24½ cents an ounce in 1932, less than one fifth of its value in 1919, a tremendous loss in thirteen years.

Three fifths of the world's population had always used silver money. It was their standard of values, as gold was in other countries. The depression in the price of silver wiped out 60 percent of their purchasing power.

The effect upon our economy was immediate. Prior to the drop in the price of silver, our Northwest was sending great cargoes of wheat, flour, and lumber to the Orient. This business ceased almost overnight. Grain rotted at the docks, and the price of wheat fell, with the drop in the price of silver, to 26 cents a bushel. England stopped buying American cotton, because her principal market for cotton cloth was the Orient and that market was now destroyed.

Warnings by sound bankers and financiers were not heeded. Actions taken to control the market boom were late, indecisive, and contradictory. A few bank failures burst the bubble.

Governments managed the depression with the same policies that caused the artificial boom—more tariffs, more price props, more rigid wage scales, more doles, more government loans to unsound creditors. The result was to retard the readjustments necessary for recovery. As the late Senator Pat McCarran of Nevada explained:

> The Great Depression dragged on for nine years because nothing was done to eliminate the causes. It was only war and the production for war that brought back full employment; and unless we propose to live perpetually in a war economy we must eliminate the causes of wars and depressions.[2]

---

2 Pat McCarran, quoted in *Senate Congressional Record*, July 29, 1953, p. 10228.

THE STORY OF FREE ENTERPRISE

A complete view of the enormously intricate forces that work together to keep our economy on an even keel is impossible for any man or group of men at any particular time. But it is apparent that there is a pattern of economic conditions that always exists prior to a depression and evidently acts to bring it on.

Mass psychology is always present in this pattern. Optimism is contagious and generates overoptimism; likewise, pessimism. We get excited and stampede in one direction. We rush to build houses, schools, office buildings, and hotels all at one time, and construction costs shoot skyward. Then suddenly we have "too many" and "too much," and construction stops. For months, you will not hear a hammer or a saw, and men walk the streets looking for work. This all causes a heavy economic loss and needless suffering.

Overoptimism and superpessimism affect an economic system mainly through the power of credit. Misuse of credit is the chief cause of inflation. Credit measures faith in the future in dollars and cents. If a banker thinks prosperity will continue for another year, he is glad to lend money for six months. If he thinks business conditions may become dull, he is reluctant to extend credit. This is where the politicians take a hand. Being anxious to keep the prosperity ball rolling, they fiercely oppose reducing the flow of credit, although the speed may be dangerously high.

Credit borrows the purchasing power of the future for the present. As we have seen, misuse of credit by the government appears in the form of inflation, which means that the supply of money in circulation is increased much faster than the supply of goods. Inflation is economic poison, an artificial economic stimulant, which brings on the feverish activity of a boom, often labeled "prosperity." During such a period, little-noticed destructive forces are built up. (These forces appear on the day that credit expansion or inflation stops or even slows down.)

The distortions caused by inflation are too numerous to note here but will be noted in another chapter. The most damaging distortion, however, is that prices rise so fast and so high that the volume of goods necessary to keep the factories running can be sold only by continued credit expansion.

Inflation speeds up spending as more and more people realize that money will buy less next week and much less next month. This process increases employment. Some costs, such as rent, wages, and interest rates, are slower to rise than are the selling prices of products. In the end, these lagging costs rise and overtake the rise in prices. In fact, they run ahead as labor unions and others discount further inflation by pushing for ever-higher wages. Businessmen and investors lose confidence in the currency. A flight of capital begins, the degenerative spiral of stagnation and unemployment is under way, and a depression is on. The depression is worsened and prolonged by governmental policies that prevent reduction of cost when inflation slows down or stops. The policies are:

1. Burdensome taxes.
2. Rigidity of industrial costs.
3. Government interference with the free market: tariffs, crop control, price control, and exchange restrictions.

What can we do to smooth out the "business cycle" of booms and busts?

Great opportunities come during depressions, but our fog of despair is so deep that few can see them.

Looking back, there is no excuse for anyone who had a little ready money during the depression of the 1930's not to be well off today. All he had to do was to buy something, almost anything—real estate, stocks, durable commodities. Andrew Carnegie was an outstanding example of those who became wealthy by buying during depressions and selling during booms. He built new steel plants during depressions. As a result, his steel company earned four times as much on its book value as did those of his competitors. If we were only to delay building that house or buying that automobile until the boom ended, we would be better off. If some 20% of us did so, the boom would not be so wild and the depression would be slight. Here again inflation exerts a destructive force; you dare not sell as money decays.

A big boom followed the end of the Korean War. Many questioned whether this was permanent prosperity or only passing improvement. Actual money in circulation increased to more than $30,000,000,000, or about $187.50 per capita. Of this, less than 6% was in coins, the balance being paper money, mostly Federal Reserve notes.

THE STORY OF FREE ENTERPRISE

One flaw in the pleasant assumption that credit is inexhaustible is that debts must be paid.

Debts are the reverse side of credit's smiling face. While the credit allowance for each resident of the United States has increased, his debt responsibility has done even better. The debit side of the national ledger shows entries of more than $600,000,000,000. More than half of the debts are owed by corporations and individuals, and the remainder by federal, state, and local governments, counties, and schools and special districts.

The per capita debt responsibility is about $3,600, a noticeable increase from a modest $64 at the turn of the century. Figuratively, everybody has cash in his pocket and a charge account.

Credit expansion cannot go on indefinitely. The experience of nations for thousands of years and the recent experiences of European nations show that it will end in a crash or paralysis. When our currency was anchored to gold and we overextended into a boom, the hawser tightened with a jerk and we crashed. After dazedly picking up the pieces, we recovered rapidly and began building another boom.

Europe shows us how to shut our eyes to threatening crashes but not how to recover after they arrive. To meet a crisis, all we have done is to cut loose from the gold standard, make our currency irredeemable, and keep on inflating. The inevitable "crash" stretches into a long state of paralysis, with wide unemployment.

The one valid remedy for chronic unemployment is to return to the free market, remove the trade barriers, and stabilize the currency. Free markets encourage investments, and there is never an overproduction of new and beautiful things at fair prices. There often is an overproduction of obsolete things of low quality priced too high.

Marx and Lenin were right about the destructive effects of inflation and its role as the chief cause of depressions. They were wrong in thinking that depressions are inherent in a free economy.

Marx and Engels said in the *Communist Manifesto* more than a century ago:

> ... Society suddenly finds itself put back into a state of momentary barbarism; it appears as if a famine, a universal war of devastation,

has cut off the supply of every means of subsistence, . . . and why? Because there is too much civilization, too much means of subsistence, too much industry, too much commerce. The productive forces at the disposal of society no longer tend to further the development of the conditions of bourgeois property; on the contrary, they have become too powerful for these conditions, by which they are fettered, and no sooner do they overcome these fetters, than they bring disorder into the whole of bourgeois society, endanger the existence of bourgeois property. The conditions of bourgeois society are too narrow to comprise the wealth created by them. And how does the bourgeoisie get over these crises? On the one hand by the enforced destruction of a mass of productive forces; on the other by conquest of new markets, and by the more thorough exploitation of the old ones. That is to say, by paving the way for more extensive and more destructive crises, and diminishing the means whereby crises are prevented.

But not only has the bourgeoisie forged the weapons that bring death to itself; it has also called into existence the men who are to wield those weapons—the modern working class—the proletarians.[3]

The Communists confidently await the next depression. They regard it as certain to come in the next few years. Their expectation is that the United States will fall like a ripe apple into their outstretched hands.

In November 1949, Georgi Malenkov, who later became premier of Russia, said in a speech before the Moscow Soviets that the long-awaited American depression was about to begin and communism would be proved to be the superior system. He was watching inflation.

Inflation is an acquired vice, no more inherent in our economic system than a craving for heroin is inherent in a normal person's metabolism.

---

3 Marx and Engels, Communist Manifesto quoted by Committee on Foreign Affairs, Sub-Committee No. 5, National and International Movements, "House Document No. 619," *The Strategy and Tactics of World Communism*, Supplement I, *One Hundred Years of Communism, 1848-1948* (U.S. Government Printing Office, Washington, D.C., 1948), p. 9.

Inflation operates mainly along with our credit structure, and credit is based upon faith and confidence. As inflation proceeds, confidence is destroyed. Thus inflation undermines its own foundations and finally takes the credit structure down with it to paralytic ruin.

Another great depression might well destroy what is left of our free economy, and Lenin's prediction might come to pass. Loss of freedom under communism would be a high price to pay for stability, the stability of stagnation, and the single alternative is political morality. Moral evils—dishonest currency manipulation, the legalized larceny of inflation, political interference with the freedom of the market, wholesale destruction of faith in ourselves and in our fellowmen—are the basic causes of depressions. And these evils are today present on a large scale.

A critical review of President Franklin D. Roosevelt's New Deal efforts to end the great depression has been made by William H. Peterson in his article "Politics of Depression."

> In 1937, the New Deal Planners' recovery program had collapsed and they had 11 million unemployed on their hands. Capital was in hiding and the country faced economic chaos indefinitely. Roosevelt accounted for the failure by saying that the bankers "had ganged up" on him.

The fact is that many of the bankers were as busy as he was.

But his economists came up with a new explanation, which was that the American economy was mature, and could not expand any more. Production capacity had reached its limit. They proved this by many charts and diagrams. They proved that the people would never again have income enough to buy all that they were able to produce, and President Roosevelt was persuaded.

Thus, despite the gains registered by private economy in 1932, the politics of depression moved from the talk stage to the action stage in 1933—with such disastrous repercussions that it is difficult even now to calculate the damage. In the name of Recovery, the New Deal confiscated the citizens' gold and broke its contractual promise to pay gold to millions of holders of Liberty Bonds—with a consequent spiraling of inflation that has engulfed us ever since. In the name of Recovery, the New Deal gave birth to an "ever-normal granary" which has turned out to be an ever-surplus, ever-subsidized abnormal granary. In the name of Recovery, the New Deal "soaked the rich" and redistributed the wealth, which dwindled for eight long years. In the name of Recovery, the New Deal legalized cartel-like business "associations" through the NRA and labor monopolies through the Wagner Act, anti-trust laws notwithstanding. In the name of Recovery, the New Deal recognized the Soviet Union, "to encourage East-West trade."

> Just before World War Two, President Roosevelt surveyed the results of depression politics—11 million persons still totally unemployed, billions added to the public debt, the nation wearying of experiment, still no magic formula to solve the depression. But politics persevered. Jim Farley reports that the president told his cabinet in late 1938: "I know who's responsible for this situation. Business, particularly the banking industry, has ganged up on me."[4]

Thus, in one sentence were dismissed the effects of a policy of unrelenting hostility to industry, the fear of inflation, super taxes, and government competition in industry.

Despite this gigantic failure, millions of voters still adhere to the belief that the New Deal was a constructive thing, particularly for the "little fellow." How this misconception was accomplished is one of the greatest lessons in politics of all time.

Schemes that arbitrarily increase the incomes of certain groups are often advanced as sure cures for depressions and guarantees of good times. The most famous of these was the Townsend Plan, proposed by Dr. Francis Townsend in 1934. It called for a pension of $200 per month for every American over 60 years of age, to be financed by a 2% federal sales tax. Certainly this plan would increase the purchasing power of a group, just as the purchasing power of a band of bank robbers is increased after a successful raid.

---

4 William H. Peterson, "Politics of Depression," *The Freeman*, March 22, 1954.

But the purchasing power of others is decreased by exactly the same amount. Further, the incentive to produce the amount of goods to be bought by those who get money for nothing is destroyed.

Real wages are lowered either by increasing prices—as by higher taxes—or by directly reducing producers' incomes.

Honest purchasing power is created by producing goods or services and selling them to obtain money to purchase other things. This is the only kind of purchasing power that creates in others an incentive to produce—and thereby fosters authentic prosperity.

Chapter Seven
MONOPOLIES

In The United States, monopolies are forbidden by numerous laws; most people believe that uncontrolled monopoly is a deadly enemy to competition and to our free-enterprise system.

Free enterprise scarcely exists outside the United States and Canada. Ninety-five percent of the people around the globe have never had any experience with a truly free economy.

"Combinations in restraint of trade," so called, are cartels, monopolies, and trusts. European countries foster the cartel system, by which producers combine, often with the government as a partner and always with its backing, to regulate trade and fix prices.

In England the tire manufacturers' cartel may prohibit a retailer from cutting prices below the cartel's fixed level or from representing one brand of tire as better than others. (In 1956 a rather timid "antitrust" law was passed which is said to prohibit price fixing.) A retailer's order for tires may be allocated among various members of the cartel, regardless of his wishes. The government gives similar power to the cartels controlling light bulbs and other articles.

Competition within a cartel is outlawed. Even if you make better tires or light bulbs, you cannot operate outside the cartel with your product. Getting into a cartel is difficult. The better your product, the more difficulty you may have.

Advocates maintain that cartels establish economic order and bring stability. The consuming public, apparently, may be disregarded. It is also held that cartels establish "economic integration" of nations, but it is a fact of history that under the cartel system entire industries were brought under the control of dictators to foster trade rivalries that contribute toward bringing about two world wars.

The Argentine government sells all the grain and meat of that country. The government of Chile sells all the copper mined there. The governments of Holland, Britain, and Belguim market natural rubber, tin, and many other products. Every ounce of materials in or out of Russia is marketed through the government.

The Sugar Act, passed by Congress in 1948, is a national cartel. This act restricts domestic production to less than 54% of our requirements, making us dependent upon foreign countries for the rest.

Despite the loss of Philippine production (900,000 tons annually) during World War II, the domestic quota was reduced "according to plan." This reduction created a critical shortage of sugar.

In 1953 the world price of sugar was around $64 a ton, the American price about $128.

The Sugar Act defines its purpose as being "to provide consumers with adequate supplies of sugar at reasonable prices."

But when the free market is not functioning, "reasonable prices" are prices at the highest level that consumers will tolerate.

Brazil offers an example of this bureaucratic thinking and its effects. That country was once the world's largest producer of sugar. The government held the prices high. Other countries started growing and exporting sugar. Brazil is now in a minor position as a sugar producer. Brazil dominated the cacao-chocolate market for many years and once had a monopoly of the world rubber market. The government had a tariff wall and export controls. Cacao seeds were smuggled out of the country to England and propagated in Kew Gardens. The young plants were distributed to Ceylon, Malaya, and the East Indies. In a few years, their production swamped that of Brazil, and chocolate became a drug on the market when government monopolies took over.

Brazil is the largest producer of coffee and for years practically monopolized world markets; the United States was the largest consumer. Millions of American housewives, unorganized and unaided by their own diplomacy-timid government, gave the coffee monopoly its worst beating.

The Brazilian government initiated price fixing and export control of coffee in 1906. In 1930, it began the practice of burning millions of bags of each year's crop surplus, which the government bought from the planters to reduce the world supply and hold up prices. In 1954 came a short crop; under artificial controls and with the help of speculators in Brazil and the United States, the retail price of coffee rose to $1.25 a pound.

Then one cup or none replaced two or three for millions of coffee drinkers, while tea and other substitutes found new customers. Consumption of the cheaper soluble coffee soared. Pledges to abstain from coffee on Wednesdays were signed by 3,000,000 New York and Brooklyn residents. The coffee rebellion became a national affair.

The market started to break early in 1955. The break depleted Brazil's gold reserve, increased the national debt, and fanned the fires of inflation. In the meantime Colombia, Venezuela, Central America, Mexico, Arabia, Africa, and even Asia had increased their production and planted more trees. If more coffee is grown than the world can drink, government monopolies will not be able to prevent consumers from benefiting by lower prices when the enlarged plantations start bearing.

Former President Peron of Argentina made fiery speeches to his countrymen blaming foreign nations for the low prices of meat and wheat and promised that he would demand higher prices. He was committed and could not lose face. Likewise, the socialized governments to which he sold could not yield and buy at the higher prices.

Peron then approached countries with partly free economies, and sold some of his wheat to individual buyers at his price. If he had lowered it a little, he would have sold more. His buyers were widely dispersed, and there was no one he could vilify.

An American corporation may be big, but it is not a monopoly. Some corporations sell more than a billion dollars' worth of goods each year, yet they are pigmies compared to the government, which collects more than $65,000,000,000 in taxes. Their economic power and conduct are limited by federal, state, and local laws and by the freedom of the people to buy what and where they please.

No corporation or government agency has an unrestricted and unlimited monopoly in the United States. The Post Office is cited as the greatest monopoly in the country, but if a shipper does not want to use letters or parcel post, he has telephone, telegraph, express or freight service available.

THE STORY OF FREE ENTERPRISE

To be effective, a private or state-owned monopoly requires the connivance or support of the government. A telephone company is a partial monopoly on the national scale and a railroad may be one in a certain area. Gas or electricity supply may be limited to a particular corporation in a city, or the city may set up its own public ownership. But in the United States none of these becomes a complete monopoly.

Federal, state, and city governments have public service commissions that tell these companies what they must or must not do to render good service at fair rates. Congress, legislatures, and city councils pass laws to restrict them.

Many industrial plants generate part of the power they consume and buy the rest from the local "monopoly." If the monopoly's price gets out of line, the factories will soon make all their own power.

Usually silent, seldom organized, and well in the background, public opinion is on the consumers' side and makes the final decisions in a free society. Politicians may grant privileges to pressure groups that promise rewards, muster votes, and provide jobs for party workers, but the fear of an aroused public is a constant preventive against the bartering away of all the public interest.

Public pressure is also exercised directly. If the public does not like the gas company's service or prices, it will buy an electric stove or refrigerator. If the price of coal goes up too far, heating plants can be converted to gas or oil. If the telephone company's toll rates are too high, the telegraph or mail can be used. If a housewife doesn't like the goods or treatment in one store, she goes to another—also she tells everybody in the neighborhood. Women can sentence the largest concern to bankruptcy or lead it to prosperity.

Patents and copyrights are monopolies. They are exceptions approved by a competitive society. The intent is that inventors and writers shall be protected from seizure of the fruits of their toil by others. Infringement of an owner's rights is a serious matter. On the other hand, a patent or a copyright is valid only for a limited number of years, and the government can control its use by the owner.

The system is not perfect and is often abused. A few companies have exploited patent monopolies. One machinery manufacturer that leased its machines to the makers of shoes was the object of antitrust action by the federal government. In one year this company had net earnings of $9.2 million. Four years later earnings declined to $5.8 million. In twenty years the common stock fell from 94 to 39. While the decline was probably due in part to the antitrust action, it was attributable largely to the company's decreased earning power, which depended mainly on patent monopolies. Ideas are difficult to monopolize, and new ideas bypass monopolies or soon render them obsolete.

Patent rights are highly important, but the policy of progressive concerns is to avoid ruthless exploitation of a patent monopoly. A business built upon patents alone is risky. A new patent may come out at any time and make older ones worthless. A widely practiced policy is to obtain licenses for the use of patents from their owners upon reasonable terms.

No concern, however large, can dam up the flow of better values and better products for industry. Developments are so fast in electronics, chemicals, atomic energy, and other fields that a company that tries to hold its position by standing still is short-sighted indeed. In years past, new inventions were often held back by those who were uncertain of their competitive value. The enlightened policy pursued today is to bring out a new product quickly and let the free market give the verdict.

Stories of new processes kept off the market are as numerous and as vague as flying saucers. One hardy perennial describes a cheap substitute for gasoline. A big oil company, never named, has allegedly bought the patent to keep the process off the market. Obviously, if the substitute were practical, the owner of the patent would soon have all the gasoline business in the world.

The DuPont company probably spends more than any other private organization on research to develop new processes. It uses them itself and offers many of them to other companies. Andrew E. Buchanan, of DuPont, explained:

> ... part of the DuPont philosophy is that if new products can be developed that offer better values to the consuming public they are sure to prosper at the expense of an older product. Therefore, since progress

is inevitable, it is better to compete with ourselves than to be put out of business by somebody else.[1]

Socialists argue that monopolies are inevitable in a competitive free economy, that large firms through greater efficiency and lower overhead costs will drive smaller ones out of business.

On the contrary, the richest possible field for a small concern is one that is dominated by a few large ones. There are advantages, along with the disadvantages, in being small. One advantage is that you can move much faster than your big competitors. The larger they get, the more like a government they become, badly tangled in red tape. The little fellow can put improvements into business much faster than the big fellows. The list of improvements made by small concerns is a long one. The big ones move more slowly because changes are much more costly. Often they are years behind the small firms.

Another important advantage of the small concern is that its personnel can be selected like a football team—every man above the average. The large concerns, with thousands of employees, must average down despite all efforts to select good men. Thus, the small concern can put "incentive management" into operation much more easily and effectively than a giant corporation can.

Because of these advantages, many large concerns buy parts from thousands of small companies. Small businesses, the fabricators, also consume the greatest part of the output of such big businesses as steel and plastics.

Small businesses (fewer than 500 employees) provide jobs for 65% of all industrial workers in the United States. With freedom assured under fair laws, the economic power of the giants is dispersed.

The decade beginning about 1900 was the "trust-building" era. The "trust-busting" era quickly followed. As the twentieth century dawned, many large concerns were being consolidated. The "steel trust" was formed of companies that produced 70% of the steel used in the country at the time.

---

1 Andrew E. Buchanan, "The Outlook in Fiber Competition," Speech before Denver Agricultural Club, Denver, Colorado, May 25, 1953 (E. I. du Pont de Nemours & Co., Wilmington, Delaware, 1953), p. 9.

The trusts were so called from the fact that many were organized by transferring a majority of each uniting company's common stock shares into the hands of trustees who managed the consolidation. This early, cumbersome arrangement was generally abandoned in favor of the single corporation—the "holding company"—which exchanged its stock for that of the merged company. Later, partly because of special taxes on dividends paid to one corporation by another, the member corporations were dissolved and the organization simplified itself into one corporation.

The later trust busters alleged, apparently with foundation, that the mergers were accomplished for the purpose of controlling the prices of the products made by the trust. Certainly they exercised a "stabilizing" influence on prices.

It was soon found, however, that mergers encouraged small competitors to grow like mushrooms. (The Bethlehem Steel Company was one mushroom.) As a result, the trusts had a hard road to travel and paid little or no dividends for years. They held a "price umbrella" over the smaller concerns. In twenty years the steel trust, which had made over half of all steel, was producing only 11%. During the depression of the 1930's, one small steel company worked twenty-four hours a day, while the large concerns ran on ruinously lean schedules.

The nucleus of the oil trust was the Standard Oil Company of New Jersey. Its organization and that of other trusts were similar to the steel trust, and their experience the same. The "natural" law worked against them, and the policy of high prices collapsed.

A hundred years before steel or oil trusts were heard of, Adam Smith pointed out:

> The price of monopoly is on every occasion the highest that can be got. The natural price, or price of free competition, on the contrary, is the lowest which can be taken, not upon every occasion indeed, but for any considerable time together.[2]

---

2 George Montgomery, *The Return of Adam Smith* (The Caxton Printers, Caldwell, Idaho, 1949), p. 109.

Trusts were not organized to win friends, and politicians soon realized that votes outweighed campaign contributions from such corporations. Supplementing the "natural law" that worked against them, Congress passed the Sherman Law forbidding price control by mergers. States passed similar laws, and trust busting was off to a flying start. The federal government has prosecuted concerns whose production was only 8% of that of the industry. It now prosecutes railroads for operating coal mines, chain stores for owning farms, and advertising agencies and many other firms for activities that are not authorized by their charters but that reduce prices for consumers.

Recently a minister bitterly attacked the "meat trust," which he designated as the "big four" packers—Armour, Cudahy, Wilson, and Swift. He charged that they control the prices of meat to consumers. Department of Agriculture figures were shown to him which demonstrated that those companies processed less than 21% of all meat consumed in the United States. The Departments of Agriculture and Justice, as well as powerful farm organizations, watch the markets closely for evidence of collusion among the four companies. Even if they did work together, it is nonsense to suppose they could control the prices of steers or meat products for very long in any locality.

An association of building contractors in an isolated area once "suggested" a price per square foot of housing that was about 20% above former competitive prices. Soon an outside contractor came in and got a number of contracts. Then others came.

Experience shows that a monopoly may control 90% or more of production and still be unable to control prices for long. The American people are opposed to cartels, monopolies, trusts, or whatever a combination against free enterprise—by management or labor—may be called.

Chapter Eight
WELFARE STATE, SOCIALISM, COMMUNISM

The Welfare state is one in which the government takes control of approximately 40% of the citizens' income and full responsibility for their welfare. The next step is the Socialist state, which supervises about 80% of a nation's income. Finally comes the Communist state, which takes over practically the entire national income.

Many well-meaning persons believe there is a "democratic socialism," which can be a barrier to communism. Not realizing where the road leads, they work for gradual socialization of the nation through a welfare state. This is a fatal fallacy, the first step to communism and governmental tyranny.

John Strachey, when minister of war in England's Social Labor government, wrote in *The Theory and Practice of Socialism:*

> It is impossible to establish Communism as the immediate successor to Capitalism. It is accordingly proposed to establish Socialism as something we can put in the place of our present decaying capitalism. Hence communists work for the establishment of Socialism as a necessary transition stage on the road to Communism.[1]

Ivor Thomas, Social Labor member of Parliament in 1945, saw the true aspects of socialism in practice and resigned from the party. He wrote in *The Socialist Tragedy:*

---

1 John Strachey, *The Theory and Practice of Socialism* (Victor Gollancz Ltd., London, 1936), p. 113.

THE STORY OF FREE ENTERPRISE

> Where there has been a decisive test the history of Europe provides no confirmation of the view that Socialism can be an effective barrier to Communism. On the contrary, the experience of many countries is that Socialism has prepared the way for Communism. Socialists have first undermined the effective barriers to Communism and when the Communists have struck at them, the Socialists have offered no effective resistance and in some cases have joined hands with the Communists.[2]

Russia came under Communist domination only after the Socialist government of Alexander Kerensky had gained power and set up a form of democratic socialism. In 1948 the platform of the Social Labor party in Britain came out frankly for Karl Marx's theories. There was no longer any pretense of social democracy.

Collectivism, under any name, means the subjugation of the individual to the group. The group may be cultural, social, economic, political, or military. The welfare state, socialism, and communism represent ascending powers of collectivism.

Socialism is a political and economic theory of social organization based on government ownership and management of the essential means of production and distribution of goods. Socialism pretends to limit itself to collective ownership of land, natural resources, and industries, but soon it takes over education to control the thinking of the people.

Communism neither pretends to limit itself to the economy of a nation nor conceals its determination to destroy religion, to spread atheism, and to control the social and cultural life of the people. It is nearly complete collectivism. Its doctrine calls for relentless abolition of private property of every description and for absolute control of the community.

And so the arrogation by a welfare state government, backed by the power of enforcement, of the right to take control of property for welfare projects is the first long step into socialism and finally into communism. It places the reins of the national economy in the hands of the government and tends to establish governmental mastery of men's minds.

---

2 Ivor Thomas, *The Socialist Tragedy* (The Macmillan Co., New York, 1951), p. 41.

Daniel Webster is said to have observed that there are men in all ages who mean to exercise power usefully; but who mean to exercise it. They mean to govern well, but they mean to govern. They mean to be kind masters, but they mean to be masters.

And the former governor of a certain state confessed:

> In these days we have to make promises that we know we cannot carry out. We have to promise the old people pensions that would bankrupt the state if we paid them. We have to promise higher salaries to the school teachers, higher wages to the working people, higher prices for the farmers, bigger allotments of public funds from the federal government. I am ashamed of what I have done but I wanted to win.

A candidate for senator advocated that old-age pensions begin at age sixty instead of sixty-five. In the 1948 presidential election, the winning Democratic candidate advocated vote-getting measures that would have created a deficit of $25 billion a year. The financial problems of the welfare state are insoluble without deficits. And deficits are the powerhouse behind inflation.

The opinion of aged Emperor Tiberius Caesar is as sound today as it was 1900 years ago. He said:

> If all poor men begin to come here and beg money for their children, individuals will never be satisfied, and the State will become bankrupt . . . In fact, it is not a request but an importunity, as utterly unreasonable as it is unforeseen, for a senator, when the house had met on other matters, to rise from his place, and pleading the number of his children, put a pressure on the delicacy of the Senate, then transfer the same constraint to myself, and, as it were, break open the exchequer, which, if we exhaust it by improper favoritism, will have to be replenished by crimes. . . . Industry will languish and idleness will be encouraged, if a man has nothing to fear, nothing to hope for from himself, and everyone, in utter recklessness, will expect

relief from others, thus becoming useless to himself and a burden to others.[3]

But welfare and free handouts quieted the populace then as they get votes today. Welfare statism finally destroyed the Roman Empire.

The psychological effect of gifts upon people able to care for themselves can be disastrous. The organization Alcoholics Anonymous has learned a significant lesson in this regard. At first it underwrote the livelihood of its AA neophytes. They were given pocket money and pay for their lodging, meals, and laundry. However, the organization found that this didn't work. It had to stop "babying" its people because it found that only one or two out of fifty, who were given a handout, came through successfully.

These experiences give further proof of two basic truths of human nature: 1, in the pursuit of happiness and peace of mind, man's spiritual growth is of paramount importance; 2, unearned handouts are habit-forming and weaken character. A political philosophy that makes its appeal through handouts or promises of cradle-to-grave security without consideration of individual effort will degrade rather than build up the human race. Ultimately it will destroy the happiness that is in store for all on earth who have made the necessary effort to earn it.

The Frenchman Alexis de Tocqueville, a brilliant student of the American Republic, with uncanny accuracy foresaw the greatest danger to its existence:

> I seek to trace the novel features under which despotism may appear in the world. The first thing that strikes the observation is an innumerable multitude of men, all equal and alike, incessantly endeavoring to procure the petty and paltry pleasures with which they glut their lives. . . .
>
> Above this race of men stands an immense and tutelary [guardian] power [the bureaucracy] which takes upon itself alone to secure their gratifications and to watch over their fate. . . .

---

3 Tiberius Caesar quoted by Tacitus. Similar version in John Jackson, *Tacitus: Histories and Annals* (Loeb Library, Heinemann, London, 1931), p. 440.

> The will of man is not shattered, but softened, bent and guided; men are seldom forced by it to act, but they are constantly restrained from acting. Such a power does not destroy, but it prevents existence; it does not tyrannize, but it compresses, enervates, extinguishes and stupefies a people, till each nation is reduced to nothing better than a flock of timid and industrious animals, of which the government is the shepherd.[4]

The welfare state promises one freedom, the freedom from responsibility, which is the only freedom a slave has.

Dr. Henry C. Link observed:

> . . . a government cannot assume responsibility for people's welfare without profoundly affecting their moral fiber. To the extent that government takes care of him, to that extent the adult citizen is deprived of the moral responsibility for himself. . . . The net result is a progressive breakdown in the moral standards of all who participate in the Welfare State. The material effect is seen in the depreciation of the dollar.[5]

The welfare state does not appeal to the man who pays his debts and returns the favors that his country has extended to him. Yet, by compulsion—plainly unconstitutional in the United States—he must take part in it. The greatest injury a nation can do to its citizens is to give them something without demanding anything in return.

Christian Economics, a magazine devoted to the material and spiritual welfare of all men, expresses the same thought:

> The attempt to transfer individual responsibility to the state by appropriations of public money and the employing of a professional bureaucracy

---

[4] Alexis de Tocqueville, *Democracy in America* (Vintage Books, Alfred A. Knopf, Inc. and Random House, Inc., New York, 1954), Vol. II, pp. 336-7.

[5] Henry C. Link, *The Way to Security* (Doubleday & Co., Garden City, New York, 1951), p. 224.

THE STORY OF FREE ENTERPRISE

is rapidly destroying the philosophy of the Good Samaritan. Fewer people have willing hearts as the state applies more coercion in the execution of its politically oriented welfare operations.

Those who are taxed heavily to support programs in which they do not believe cannot possibly have willing hearts. Warm, human sympathy and kindliness are dissipated by the cold-blooded force with which the state deprives them of the fruits of their labor. They come to dislike those to whom the benefits are given because they rightly suspect that political pressure rather than need is the determining factor.

Those who receive the largess soon consider it their right—that society owes it to them regardless of their own efforts and their own worth. Many who subsist partially or in full at public expense see no reason to exert themselves. Most people who are forcibly despoiled of the fruits of their efforts grow discouraged and refrain from exerting themselves to maximum capacity. Production, therefore, declines, and there is less for all.[6]

Brooks Atkinson of *The New York Times*, after living in Moscow with the government-planned economy of the Soviet Union, wrote:

> There is a calculated risk in everything. There has been a calculated risk in every stage of American development. The nation was built by men who took risks—pioneers who were not afraid of the wilderness, businessmen who were not afraid of failure, scientists who were not afraid of truth, thinkers who were not afraid of progress, dreamers who were not afraid of action.[7]

It is incredible that our nation, with an economic system that has given it by far the highest standard of living on earth, and the utmost security and safety, should deliberately destroy that system and substitute for it one

---

6 *Christian Economics*, New York, June 16, 1953, p. 2.
7 Brooks Atkinson, *Once Around the Sun* (Harcourt, Brace & Co., New York, 1952). Letter to Mrs. Robert Cruise McManus, August 28, 1962.

that is followed by nations, now weak and helpless, that are begging us for assistance. But it is happening.

We have been warned by the most serious thinkers of the time that socialism means slavery. We have had it proved before our eyes in England, Germany, France, Italy, Russia, and other countries. Under England's Social Labor government, workers could not leave their jobs without the state's permission. A slave is one who has no economic liberty—he cannot leave his job without his master's consent. In spite of warnings and examples, our welfare state grows, moving steadily toward socialism.

Maxwell Anderson, the playwright, wrote:

> The power of government in the United States has grown like a fungus in wet weather. Price supports and unemployment benefits and farm subsidies are the rule, not the Exception. Our government has turned into a giant giveaway program, offering far more for votes than was ever paid by the most dishonest ward-heeler. We march steadily toward the prefabricated state. Yet we see clearly that in England, socialism turns rapidly into communism, and that in Russia and Yugoslavia, communism gives neither freedom nor security. The guaranteed life turns out to be not only *not* free—it's not safe.[8]

The welfare state is a parasite, feeding upon the economic system by taxes and inflation. Its advocates do not pretend that it will wither away; they constantly work to expand its activities. Its most effective appeal is the offer of security.

It sells protection, but at monopolistic prices. So we have government agencies that make loans to farmers and that carry out farm price supports, social security, federal housing, federal electric power, federal irrigation projects, federal control of banking with arbitrarily low interest rates.

---

8 Maxwell Anderson, *The Guaranteed Life* (Foundation for Economic Education, Inc., Irvington-on-Hudson, New York, 1950), pp. 9-10.

The collectivists argue that natural resources, particularly water power and oil, belong to "all the people." They oppose any "grab" of these natural resources by "greedy spoilsmen," "sefish private interests," and "giveaways." They call these natural resources "the people's heritage," "the people's treasurehouse," "God's gift to the people."

Welfare statists raised an uproar when title to the tidewater oil lands was returned to the states in 1954. They argued that the people's resources should be developed by the federal government instead of by the *people*, who have done it successfully since the nation was founded.

The founders of the republic knew better. They knew that all primary wealth comes from the earth. If it is true that any *one* of the earth's natural resources belongs to the people and therefore must be owned and operated by the government, the argument should be applied to *all* the earths resources. If the tidewater oil lands of Texas and the water power of the Colorado belong to the government, then why not the coal fields of West Virginia and Pennsylvania, the gas fields of Texas, the forests of Oregon, the sulphur beds of Louisiana, and the rich farm lands of the prairie states? Why play favorites with water power and oil, and leave out forests, mines, land and its production of food? As more of the economic wealth comes to "belong to the people" by government ownership and operation, the more votes the government has, and the fight against statism is difficult and never-ending. This is the road that has no stop sign until it reaches its final conclusion—communism.

The seductiveness of the welfare state was well described by Gibbon in *The Decline and Fall of the Roman Empire:*

> Augustus was sensible that mankind is governed by names; nor was he deceived in his expectation, that the senate and the people would submit to slavery, provided they were respectfully assured that they still enjoyed their ancient freedom. A feeble senate and enervated people cheerfully acquiesced in the pleasing illusion.[9]

---

9 Edward Gibbon, *Decline and Fall of the Roman Empire* (Chatto & Windus, London, 1960), p. 40.

Rome and its glory passed.

We have been given step-by-step instructions by Earl Browder on building communism by peaceful methods. "Don't startle the people, soothe them with sweet phrases, no force until you have them" is the policy.

Some of the steps that Mr. Browder enumerates for deluding and enslaving a free people are steps our government has taken in building a welfare state. With admirable frankness Browder calls them "key points" in the Communist program:

> Social security legislation
> Government work projects
> Unemployment insurance
> Federal health program
> Federal housing program
> Restriction of monopolies
> Stock-exchange control
> Federal development of water supplies [natural resources]
> Control of banking and credit systems
> Guaranteed production cost for farmers
> Federal marketing of surplus crops abroad[10]

All of these have the common feature of being particular aspects of the tendency to concentrate in the hands of the state the reins of natural economy—they aid the growth of *state capitalism*.

The welfare state is unstable because it is a stage of transition. It leads to insecurity of property, which is invariably followed by relaxation of industry and by unemployment, which calls for more and more government intervention until finally a simple arbitrary government is established.

---

10 Earl Browder, *Social and National Security* (Workers Library Publishers, New York, 1938), pp. 20-22. [These steps are paraphrased and condensed from the original text.]

The German Empire was the first modern welfare state. It created a regimented people. The empire was destroyed and the Third Reich, on the same foundation of the omnipotent-state concept, followed.

Upon the rubble, and with our help, the Germans have erected a nearly free economy which promises to be the strongest in Europe.

We have the Constitutional liberty to destroy our own liberty. Once it is destroyed in a modern state and despotism is established, it appears to be impossible for a people ever to regain freedom by their own efforts. Deliverance must come from the outside. We were the liberators of England, France, Italy, Belgium, Norway, Holland, Denmark, and Germany. Where is the power that can save us?

The final decision to barter away our liberty for socialism will be made, if not by us, by those who are of school age now. If the matter were voted on today, socialism could not win. There are only about a million socialist votes, yet socialism is well established under the thin disguise of the welfare state.

The Fallacy of "Federal Aid"

Proponents of federal aid maintain that only the federal government is able to finance services needed by states and individuals. The fact is that none of the 50 states is in as deplorable financial condition as is the federal government. Yet, in 1955, the governors of two of the richest states in the union, New York and Michigan, agreed that their states needed more federal aid.

Under our Constitution the federal government has no powers that are not granted to it by the states; neither does the federal government have any wealth that is not taken from the 50 states.

As an example, in 1952 that state of Indiana paid $1,359 million to the federal government. It got back less than $73 million, or about five percent.

In the same year Indiana paid into the Federal Aid to the States Fund of the U.S. Treasury $72,483,000 and got back in State Aid grants $38,089,000. Federal brokerage cost Indiana $34,394,000—over 47 percent.

One writer has said:

> The people in your states need some aid. So we are going to tax them, bring the money to Washington, deduct the expenses of administering the aid, and then provide the aid they need with their own money.
>
> It is just as if a doctor said to his patient: "You need a blood transfusion. I am going to take some blood out of your left arm; I am going to put it back in your right arm. I will spill some in the process, but I am going to give you a blood transfusion with your own blood."

The government does not create wealth; in fact it is a great consumer of wealth, all of which it must take from the states, but it does have means of getting *money* which are prohibited to the states, namely, levying hidden taxes, borrowing money from the Federal Reserve System, and printing more currency. All are inflationary.

By far the largest and worst of these is bank-credit inflation, whereby a dollar of government deficit can become the basis for six dollars or more of bank-credit expansion. By this means, much of the wealth belonging to the citizens of the states is removed from their control. The federal government is made to seem a source of great wealth.

There are 46 states less wealthy than New York and Michigan. New York bears 15 percent of the federal tax burden, Michigan nearly 6 percent, hence the aid given to those two states must come from the 48 states that pay the 79 percent; these also are candidates for federal aid. Consequently, a request for federal aid means that the states are begging from each other. Wouldn't the best possible form of aid the federal government could give to any state be simply to economize in its own expenditures, "so that the states may be lightly burdened"? Federal grants-in-aid are fundamental to the establishment of American socialism.

Chapter Nine
INFLATION—THE LURE TO RUIN

Because of the political necessity of bidding billions of dollars for votes, it seems to be impossible to balance the budget of the welfare state.

The housewife and worker complain of high prices. Businessmen and financiers call it inflation. The economic evil is the same, whatever its name. Our nation faces the gravest peril in its history, and we are taking great doses of this economic poison.

Our survival depends upon our economic strength. The Federal Reserve Board reports:

> Unless inflation is controlled, it could prove to be an even more serious threat to the vitality of our country than the more spectacular aggressions of enemies outside our borders.[1]

Harry F. Byrd, former chairman of the Senate Finance Committee, said:

> Our fiscal crisis at home is just as serious as our military crisis abroad. We cannot meet the military crisis without preservation of our free enterprise productive system, and we cannot preserve that system in fiscal insolvency.[2]

Former President Eisenhower said:

---

[1] William McChesney Martin, Speech upon taking oath of office as Chairman, Board of Governors, Federal Reserve System, April 2, 1951.
[2] Harry F. Byrd, Letter to Mrs. Robert C. McManus, August 7, 1962.

> I firmly believe that the army of persons who urge greater centralization of authority and greater dependence upon the Federal Treasury are really more dangerous to our form of government than any external threat that can possibly be arrayed against us.[3]

Lord Keynes wrote:

> Lenin is right. The process engages all the hidden forces of economic law on the side of destruction, and does it in a manner that not one man in a million is able to diagnose.[4]

At first, inflation gives to a government the aura of omnipotence. When our government had not a dime it did not owe, in 1954, it continued to spend billions of dollars. It built great dams, water-power plants, and vast irrigation projects. Where did the money come from?

The government simply printed some bonds and some notes and ran them into the banks, and *presto!* new bank credits appeared as the government's "deposits" and much new cash—paper money—appeared also. So the federal debt was increased and the money supply also increased. The purchasing value of the dollar went down to 52 cents. In the year ending May 5, 1955, money actually in circulation was $29,782,000,000 and the stock of gold in Fort Knox was $21,671,000,000.

In 1939, the federal debt was limited to $45,000,000,000. It was $1,191,000,000 in 1915. Successive rises in seven years of Franklin Roosevelt's administration, including four war years, brought it to $275,000,000,000 in 1946. In a few more years, the limit was reached. In the twenty years following 1931, receipts were greater than expenditures in only three years, 1947, 1948, and 1951. In other years, money was borrowed to meet the deficit.

---

3 Dwight D. Eisenhower, letter to Congressman Ralph W. Gwinn, June 7, 1949, quoted in "Where Eisenhower Stands on Sixteen Vital Issues," p. 18.
4 John Maynard Keynes, *The Economic Consequences of the Peace* (Harcourt, Brace & Co., New York, 1920), p. 236.

THE STORY OF FREE ENTERPRISE

President Eisenhower asked for another $15,000,000,000 increase in the limit and Congress granted a temporary $6,000,000,000 increase to expire June 30, 1955.

The statutory limit does not cover all the federal debt; this is less than half of the over-all national debt, including the debts of state and local governments, corporations, and individuals. In 1955 the Department of Commerce reported $64,250,000,000 in additional federal debts outside the limit; most of this was owed to its own agencies—I.O.U.'s in Social Security funds are one instance.

The Department estimated federal debt as $294,400,000,000 gross, or $230,200,000,000 net; state and local, $37,900,000,000 gross, or $33,400,000,000 net; corporations, $208,800,000,000 gross, or $176,600,000,000 net, and individuals, $165,300,000,000 gross or $165,300,000,000 net. The total national debt, public and private, came to $706,400,000,000 gross, or $605,500,000,000 net. Today it is far beyond that amount.

A cheering forecast was given in 1955 by Gordon W. McKinley, chief economist of the Prudential Insurance Company. He estimated that the nation's gross national income of $356,000,000,000, about half of what it owed, would rise to $540,000,000,000 in ten years and that personal income would increase from $285,000,000,000 to $420,000,000,000.

But the Committee on Federal Tax Policy reports that federal expenditures equaled 3 percent of total national production in 1930, 10 percent in 1940, 14 percent in 1950, and 21 percent in 1954. The federal government has become the world's largest business. In terms of value, it is the biggest landlord and tenant, the biggest owner of grazing and timberlands, of food supplies, warehouses, sea and air passenger transport, power plants, and retail stores. In addition, it has more than one hundred lending agencies to finance private ventures. It has two and a half million civilian employees, while city, county, and state governments raise the figure to six and a half million—one of every nine workers in the country. The Eisenhower administration eliminated some competition with private business, but new lines started. As Senator Byrd said: "One slips in as a mouse and soon becomes an elephant."[5]

---

5 Harry F. Byrd, letter to Mary Borden McManus, August 24, 1962.

Money has become an elastic measure of value. Ever since rulers discovered the power that control of money gives them over the people, there have been three parties in every trade—producer, consumer, and government. If a dealer cuts his yardstick to eighteen inches or sells eight ounces of butter for a pound, the government tosses him into jail. But the government cuts the cents in a dollar from 100 to 49 and seems immune to national and moral laws. The process is called inflation—the *value* of the dollar undergoes *deflation*, the *number* of dollars in circulation is *inflated*.

Its thousands of publicity agents and tons of literature give the impression that producers are responsible for high prices. Everybody knows that in this machine age the farmer produces more grain with less work than ever before and the efficiency of the factories rapidly increases, but inflation robs the producers of much of the benefit of the increasing power of production.

In a desperate effort to control inflation, some foreign governments have established "commodity money"—paper certificates stating that they are exchangeable for certain amounts of grain and other commodities. But the temptation to inflate the issue of commodity money has always proved irresistible, and soon the total amount of this paper money has far exceeded the amount of commodities.

The problem of inflation involves the old law of supply and demand. When production and consumption are balanced, the market is stable. A third element in this market is money, the measure of value which the government produces and monopolizes. When the money supply is arbitrarily increased, prices rise. Money, being more plentiful, acts as any commodity does—it becomes cheaper. Cheap money is the cause, not the effect, of high prices. When the money supply is increased, the value is debased, and high prices follow immediately.

A revealing survey of Federal Reserve, life-insurance, and government sources was made by Colonel E. C. Harwood, director of the American Institute for Economic Research. Covering the years from 1939 to 1952, it was a nationwide tabulation of insurance, bank deposits, government savings bonds, and Social Security reserves.

He found that the holders of these so-called securities had lost a staggering total of $158,000,000,000 through inflation or depreciation of the dollar. Some 88,000,000 holders of life insurance found that the purchasing value of their policies was $97,300,000,000 less than they had expected. Government bonds had depreciated $21,500,000,000 from their illusory face value. The Social Security "reserve" had shrunk by $7,400,000,000—almost half.

Many government advisers recommend price and wage controls as a cure for inflation. But this merely provides more government interference in the chaos it already has brought to the normal operation of economic laws.

The Committee for Economic Development reports:

> Experience in the United States and in other countries has demonstrated that general price and wage controls and rationing is not an effective solution to inflation. Even while controls are in effect, price increases break through in black markets, in deterioration of quality, and in the disappearance of low-priced goods. Prices and wages are then determined in a political bargaining process which favors the most powerful politically. This constant leapfrogging of prices and wages has disastrous effects on the security of the nation. And when the controls finally come to an end, the dammed-up inflationary pressure breaks out in open inflation.[6]

On the last day of 1776, the State of Rhode Island and Providence Plantations passed a wage-and-price-ceiling law. Top prices in those nostalgic days were fixed as follows: milk, 9¢ a gallon; one pound of tobacco or a night's lodging, 5¢; shaving by a barber, 3½¢, and a carpenter's wage, 70¢ a day.

Similar laws followed in other states until the American Continental Congress, in 1788, adopted this formal resolution:

> It hath been found by experience that limitation of the prices of commodities is not only ineffective for the purpose proposed,

---

[6] The Research and Policy Committee of the Committee for Economic Development, *Paying for Defense*, A statement on National Policy, November 1950, p. 5.

but likewise productive of very evil consequences, to the great detriment of the public service and grievous oppression of all individuals.[7]

In 1585, when the Duke of Parma invaded Belgium, the city of Antwerp decreed price controls on almost everything. Hailed as a stroke of political genius, the decree proved to be a fatal military blunder. People inside the city quickly bought all the food, and peasants outside would not bring in more at low prices. Antwerp fell from its own stupid economic blockade.

In 301 A.D., as recorded by the historian Lactantius, the Emperor Diocletian fixed wage rates and maxium prices on beef, grain, eggs, clothing, and all other articles of general consumption in the Roman Empire. Many Romans were put to death before the edict was repealed. The emperor abandoned his throne to live in a cabbage patch and brood over his folly.

Not learning from experience, the Emperor Julian only sixty years later abolished the free market and tried to fix prices. The pattern of failure was the same.

Athens, 400 years before the Christian era, put ironclad price controls on grain. As they do today, an army of government inspectors spread over the country to police every transaction. "Parity prices" were not known then, instead of growing a surplus which the government could not give away, Greek peasants stopped raising grain, and disaster followed.

The Emperor Hammurabi of Babylon, a headliner in 2200 B.C., imposed a code which controlled all wages, prices, rents, and land boundaries. Irrigation was a state monopoly. Babylon, its economy smothered, declined until it became only a memory and a warning.

In our age, the Soviet dictatorship leads in trying to ignore the free market. When Stalin was living, the government planning board set the same price for a ton of grain, a ton of bread, and a ton of cotton. The

---

[7] *Journals of the Continental Congress, 1774-1789* (U.S. Government Printing Office, Washington, D.C., 1908), Vol. XI, p. 569.

Central Committee of the Communist Party met and Stalin announced: "This will ruin the cotton growers and leave us without cotton."

Stalin knew that processing and baking raise the price of bread above that of raw grain and that the production cost of cotton is greater than that of grain. He learned that not from his own arbitrary market but from the world price system which the Soviet Union tries to destroy.

Donald R. Richberg, a New Deal stalwart until he lost his enthusiasm for government planning of the economy, wrote:

> Our real choice lies between a state-controlled economy, a political tyranny or political freedom. There is no half-way house except a poor shelter where one may pause on the way to his permanent abode, in a land of masters and servants, or in a land of free men.[8]

How Inflation Works

Inflation, which builds up forces that threaten to destroy our economic system, is accomplished very easily. The government prints bonds and notes and sells them to the banks. This puts more paper money and, most important, more bank credit into circulation. The money supply and the national debt increase together.

Now, when the government borrows $100 from Jimmy Jones by selling him a bond which Jones pays for out of his savings, the government's power to purchase is increased by $100, and Jones's power is decreased by $100—and there is no inflation.

But something very different happens when the government borrows from a commercial bank. The bank simply makes an entry on its books crediting the United States with the loan, and the United States government issues checks against its credit at the bank. Those who receive the checks usually deposit them in a bank, so the total money supply has been increased. As this unearned fiat credit circulates in the channels of trade,

---

8 Donald R. Richberg, "Where Is Organized Labor Going?," *Harvard, Business Review*, July, 1949, p. 411.

it falsifies every price indicator it touches. Eventually it reaches them all. The resulting inflationary distortion is a maker of depressions.

Over 90% of the business of this nation is done with checks against bank credit. Thus it becomes clear that an agency that can create or control *new* bank credit is just as well off as if it came into complete control of so much money.

Here is the financial statement of a typical bank:

RESOURCES

Cash and Due from banks	$ 4,361,380.23
United States Government Securities	7,262,442.30
State and Municipal Bonds	626,512.56
Loans and Discounts	6,002,917.53
Federal Reserve Bank Stock	33,000.00
Real Estate	1.00
Fixtures and Equipment	86,520.32
Cash Value of Life Insurance	17,887.13
Other Resources	4,777.59
	$18,395,438.66

LIABILITIES

Capital stock	$ 300,000.00
Surplus	800,000.00
Undivided Profits	256,792.38
Reserves	41,514.61
Deposits	16,997,131.67
	$18,395,438.66

The statement does not give the actual cash that is in the bank. The cash is included in the item "cash and due from banks." However, it may safely be said that this bank probably does not have over $400,000 in cash at any particular time except, perhaps, under special conditions, as when Christmas Club checks are issued.

The amount of credit a bank can issue or money it can loan depends upon its "capital structure." The capital structure is the par value of the capital stock plus undivided profits plus surplus.

Nearly all banks are members of the Federal Reserve System. The Federal Reserve banks, as the name indicates, were created as a reserve for emergencies of member banks. A true reserve is an amount of capital retained by banks to meet probable emergency demands. The banks buy stock in the Federal Reserve banks, thus transferring a portion of their capital assets to Federal Reserve. Originally the Federal Reserve banks were designed to be *only* reserve banks, places of *final resort* for bank credit. As it has worked out, particularly for borrowings by the government, they have become the banks of *first resort*, a convenient device for complete governmental manipulation of money and credit. The government can change the reserve regulations to suit its own convenience as a borrower at any time.

This is one instance of how the government operates: In one year, the Treasury offered two bond issues. The first one was for $3 billion, with interest of 2¾%. These bonds were to be exchanged for the people's savings. Banks were not permitted to buy them. But only a third of the bonds were sold, indicating clearly that the interest rate was not high enough to induce the people to exchange their savings for the bonds. This bond issue was not inflationary, because it did not increase the money supply. Every dollar that was subscribed for the bonds came out of some person's savings.

Soon the Treasury put out another bond issue with the lower rate of 2⅜%. It was promptly oversubscribed, *because the banks were permitted to buy*. This issue was plain inflation of the kind that already had reduced the buying power of the dollar by nearly one half. The issue increased the money supply by adding both to bank credit and to paper money in circulation. How? The bonds bore a higher rate of interest than much government paper the banks had in their portfolios. Banks could buy to the limit of the regulations. If their cash reserves ran low, all they had to do was to sell some of the lower interest-bearing certificates of indebtedness to a Federal Reserve bank and receive crisp, newly printed paper money in return. This operation was profitable for the banks.

In another week the Treasury sold $1,200,506,000 of 91-day treasury bills bearing an interest rate of 1⅝%. This issue also was promptly oversubscribed by the banks. Previous to the offering, however, the "money market was eased" by the Federal Reserve System's buying $600,000,000 of certificates of indebtedness from the banks. This built up the banks' reserve cash and put them in a "receptive position" for the treasury bills.

The government must borrow from the banks because it spends more than it receives in taxes. The difference is the deficit—the pressure behind inflation.

The system can be tersely explained: When the banks take a billion dollars of government bonds, they credit the United States Treasury with a billion dollars and charge their government bond account with a billion dollars, or, they create by a bookkeeping entry the money with which to buy the bonds.

Inflation has been called "legalized counterfeiting." It is also called a "pocket-picking tax." The counterfeiting hides from the law. The Treasury and Federal Reserve System openly dictate the financial welfare or ruin of every citizen.

Inflation is a tax, the cruelest form of taxation ever devised. It robs the widows and orphans of part of their life insurance and annuities. It robs the thrifty of the value of their savings. It robs the aged of the security and independence for which they have worked in their productive years. It works while you sleep. It filches away part of the value of your money and "securities" without going near your wallet or your safety-deposit box. Its cruel power provides "pie in the sky" for millions of people, and handouts that are received under the illusion that nobody pays for them. It is clearly immoral. It is a political means for distributing wealth.

You have to be in a country in the final stages of inflation to realize the extent of national degradation. When a French businessman was asked what the French intended to do about inflation, he said: "We live from day to day. We have lost faith in man and God. We don't want to think about it or talk about it."

France, like other countries, does not learn from its own experiences. John Law and his Mississippi Bubble, which bankrupted the country in the 1720's, are forgotten. The assignats, which came seventy years later, were the wildest debauchery in worthless paper money until the speculation in German marks after World War I. The assignats started as a modest issue of notes guaranteed by land which the state had confiscated from the nobility and the church. The money was soon squandered and more issues followed. Price controls and other repressive measures, with the death penalty for evaders, came next. Starvation, unemployment, and chaos brought a dictator.

An irredeemable currency, such as we have in the United States today, is a dishonest currency. This dishonesty contaminates all the people. In 1933, the government abolished our freedom to exchange a dollar of paper money for gold. That is why our currency is irredeemable. We do not have the freedom to express our confidence in our government by buying or selling gold.

Look at the paper money in your pocket. There may be a silver certificate among the bills, but probably most of them are Federal Reserve "notes." Each $5 bill has printed on it "The United States of America will pay to the bearer on demand five dollars." Suppose you present the note at the bank and ask to exchange it for five dollars. The teller may think you have lost your mind. So far as he knows, your Federal Reserve note *is* five dollars. Perhaps, if you present it at a Federal Reserve Bank and insist, they will give you another note just like it (except for the serial number) or perhaps—if not too many are presented—a silver certificate.

Philip McKenna, president of the Gold Standard League, told our Senate:

> On March 6, 1933, the clock was turned back to the bad days two centuries or more ago when kings or dictatorships maintained that it was their exclusive prerogative to seize the money of the people and to reissue coins of less value or sometimes only paper as their whims or needs dictated.[9]

---

9 Philip M. McKenna, Statement to 83rd Congress, Second Session, March 29, 30, 31 and April 1, 1954 (Hearings before a Subcommittee of the Committee on Banking and Currency, United States Senate on S. 13, S. 2332, S. 2364, S. 2514), p. 275.

An irredeemable currency system makes inflation easy. Inflation is the most potent device known, other than the use of military force, for a government to win control of a people and subject it to tyranny. Wherever one finds dictatorial governments, one also finds irredeemable currency or a military force at the disposal of the dictator.

A redeemable currency is the greatest friend a free people can have; it is the most potent weapon against governmental tyranny.

One of the most dangerous aspects of an irredeemable currency is that it is a subtle device not understood by the people. Once given a taste of easy money, they will clamor for more and more and, like the drug addict, will employ every argument the human mind can devise to retain it.

On December 3, 1861, Abraham Lincoln warned us, "Political power if surrendered will surely be used to close the door of advancement and to fix new disabilities and burdens until all of liberty shall be lost."

Power-seeking politicians always have been awake to the use of irredeemable currency for deceiving and controlling the people. Our government has a supply of gold more than adequate to permit redeemability, yet it has revealed no intention of making plans to redeem its bills of credit. Indeed, it has opposed all efforts to obtain provisions for redemption.

Professor Spahr, a writer on economics, asked:

> What valid basis has our government for depriving our people of their right to own gold or other natural property? What defense does our government have for selling gold to foreigners but refusing to redeem its own paper held by its own citizens? Administration of the people's money shows moral bankruptcy.[10]

Professor Donald L. Kemmerer of the University of Illinois also questions the legality of our country's discrimination between foreigners and its own citizens.

---

10 Walter E. Spahr, *Our Irredeemable Currency System* (Economists' National Committee on Monetary Policy, New York, 1950). [Paraphrase of original material.]

Andrew Dickson White summarizes the fallacy of inflation in his "Fiat Money Inflation in France":

> They [the French] had then learned [in John Law's time] how easy it is to issue it [currency], how difficult it is to check its overissue; how seductively it leads to the absorption of the means of the workingmen and men of small fortune; how heavily it falls on all those living on fixed incomes, salaries or wages; how securely it creates on the ruin of prosperity of all men of meager means a class of debauched speculators, the most injurious class that a nation can harbor—more injurious indeed than professional criminals whom the law recognizes and can throttle; how it stimulates overproduction at first and leaves every industry flaccid afterwards; how it breaks down thrift and develops political and social immorality. All this, France has been thoroughly taught by experience.
>
> It was no mere attempt at theatrical display, but a natuural impulse, that led a thoughtful statesman during a debate, to hold up a piece of that old paper money and declare that it was stained with the blood and tears of their fathers.[11]

Comte Gabriel Mirabeau, in the debates on the assignats, declared, in 1790:

> Paper money is a nursery of tyranny, corruption and delusion; the veritable debauch of authority in delirium.[12]

And Talleyrand said:

> You can, indeed, arrange it so that the people shall be forced to take a thousand livres in paper instead of a thousand livres in specie; but you can never arrange it so that a man shall be obliged to give a thousand

---

[11] Andrew Dickson White, "Fiat Money Inflation in France," *The Freeman* (Pamphleteers, Inc., Los Angeles, California, 1945), pp.9-10.
[12] Comte Gabriel Mirabeau quoted by Andrew Dickson White, *Ibid.*, p. 15.

livres in specie for a thousand livres in paper—in that fact is imbedded the entire question; and on account of that fact the whole system failed.[13]

Daniel Webster summed it up in one sentence which he is reported to have made:

Of all the contrivances for cheating the laboring classes of mankind, none has been more effective than that which deludes them with paper money.

---

13 Talleyrand quoted by Andrew Dickson White, *Ibid.*, p. 20.

Chapter Ten
SOCIALIZED SECURITY

Except perhaps for confirmed gamblers, everybody wants some kind of security. Man wants it for today and for those future years when his earning power is ended by age or disability.

We must reconcile ourselves to the fact that nothing within the range of human power can provide absolute security. This rule applies equally to individuals, nations, and the entire world. Since the security of the government depends on individuals, it should be evident that large numbers of individuals cannot provide their own security by becoming public charges.

Although there are no distinct lines, we are divided into three classes:

1. the thrifty, those who are able and willing to provide for themselves and their dependents in disability and old age;
2. the improvident, those who are able but unwilling to provide for their dependents or themselves in old age;
3. the indigent, those who are unable to provide for their dependents or themselves.

The majority of us seem to believe that it is the duty of the government to compel class 2, the improvident, to provide for their dependents and themslves and to assist class 1 in taking care of class 3.

Formerly this task was left to local and state authorities, but the idea spread that the federal government could do it better, and a Social Security law was passed in 1935. This law did seem to encourage and require class 2 to provide for themselves and their dependents, as well as to assist in the rehabilitation of many of class 3.

In 1939 the law was superseded by another which made all three classes into one—public charges, wards of the state.

Now, millions of people hold the following beliefs:

1. Social Security is an insurance system run by the federal government that guarantees most American families against loss of income by reason of old age or death or disability of the head of the family;
2. the workers pay for this insurance with premiums held out of their wages, with a like amount paid by their employers;
3. these premiums build up rights to benefits for workers and their families;
4. the amount of the benefits depend upon the workers' paid premiums;
5. these premiums go into a vast reserve fund, where they draw interest, and the promised benefits will be paid out of the reserve fund as they are being paid now;
6. these benefits are not relief. You get what you pay for, and you pay for what you get;
7. the government does not have the right to alter, amend, or cancel the insurance or any part of it at any time, for any reason or for no reason, without the consent of the insured and without returning paid premiums. The insured has certain rights under law, and the government cannot withdraw consent to such legal action or prevent a court from hearing any suit against the government.

All the foregoing beliefs are false.

From January 1, 1950, to January 1, 1955, the federal government collected $18,965,000,000 in social security taxes and paid out benefits totaling $11,716,000,000. As far back as the end of March 1955 the "reserve fund" contained $20,400,000,000 *in government I.O.U.'s* or bonds. This reserve is not an asset. It cost taxpayers $500,000,000 in interest charges, and eventually all these bonds must be paid by additional taxation.

The chief actuary of the Social Security Administration stated that it would take $35,000,000,000 to pay the claims of the people now receiving benefits. The Secretary of the Treasury testified in July 1955 that "under the present provisions of collections and disbursements the old age survivors' insurance system is actuarially unsound." Congressmen estimate that in 1975 it will require $20,000,000,000 a year in taxes to meet the social security payments so far promised. The "premiums" exacted by Social Security are not contributions paid voluntarily; they are taxes collected under penalties. Benefits are not definite and they may be changed whenever the Congress wishes.

Why the compulsion in social security?

If it is an insurance system, why force people into it?

The federal social-security system is actually a tax on the present generation to pay for current government expenses in exchange for a promise that a future generation will tax itself to supply retirement annuities for those now paying the social-security tax. That generation will have to pay the cost of government in its day as we do now. In addition, it will have to pay for our annuities. That is grossly unfair on our part. It is an effort to steal from our descendants. We are not striving to make life easier for them, we are placing an unbearable burden upon them.

What moral right has one generation to levy an ever-increasing burden on succeeding generations? It is more honorable to be able to say, as did a very wise man of long ago, "Neither did we eat any man's bread for naught, but wrought with labor and travail night and day, that we might not be chargeable to any of you" (St. Paul's epistle to the Thessalonians III:8).

The present social-security law promises this generation the same benefits for which we are being taxed to provide for others. The same law will tax our children twice as much to pay for our benefits. The next generation of wage earners may find that the financial burden we have bequeathed to them is too great, and they may have the votes to do something about it.

Many politicians believe that to oppose social security is to commit political suicide. But in 1950 Congressman Noah H. Mason of Illinois said:

> . . . revenue today collected through the social-security tax goes to meet the ordinary expense of the Government, and that means that a

substantial part of future social-security costs will have to be met out of future tax revenues.

> . . . I wonder if that scheme of taxing again the children and grandchildren of the social-security beneficiary for something he and his employer are supposed to have paid for—but Uncle Sam has spent the receipts from the social-security tax for other things—can be called anything but dishonest and immoral, a Ponzi-type shell game that has been sold to the American taxpayer as a plan to provide security in his old age.[1]

It is not true that the social-security funds that are deducted from pay checks and contributed by employers go into a reserve fund to be paid out later. The original Federal Social Security Act was approved by the United States Court in 1937 as an exercise of the Constitutional taxing power of the Congress *for the benefit of the general fund of the United States Treasury*. The Court has held[2] that the Congress has no constitutional power to earmark or segregate any kind of tax proceeds for certain purposes. Congress can continue to collect the social-security payroll taxes and may pay out whatever it desires as benefit payments.

Another deception is the representation of social-security taxes as insurance premiums for the right to get back specified benefits at a specified time. On the contrary, the social-security law carries the provision, "The right to alter, amend or appeal any provision of this act is hereby reserved to the Congress."

The terms "insurance" and "annuities" canot be applied in their usual sense.

No one now troubles to pretend that the introductions of new bills to liberalize the Social Security program are anything but political maneuvers. Both political parties extoll its merit and vie with each other to "liberalize" the benefits in election years. All the voter has to decide is which candidate promises more.

---

1 Noah M. Mason, *Congressional Record*, Appendix, February 27, 1950, p.A1535.
2 Helvering *vs.* Davis, U.S. 619.

Social Security operates with little pretense of balancing its budget. The taxes are haphazard, the spending and promise more so. There is little relation between the money to be raised and that which is promised.

The present law penalizes persons over 65 years of age for working. They are penalized for adding to the general wealth of the nation and themselves. The amount they may earn while receiving social-security payments is strictly limited by law.

Social Security makes everyone a ward of the government, destroys personal responsibility and incentive, and is an agent in the process of economic leveling.

A publication of the Social Security Administration says:

> Social Security and Public Assistance Programs are a basic essential for attainment of the socialized state envisaged in democratic ideology, a way of life which so far has been realized only in light measure.[3]

Probably the majority of the people favor the concept of a program to relieve the needy to aid and encourage the self-supporting to provide for themselves. Certainly they do not approve of putting everybody on relief.

Wholesale bidding for votes by forcing everyone into Social Security and "liberalizing" the benefits by reducing the age limits and increasing the payments will make over our lives, socialize our government and economy, and redistribute our wealth by many billions of dollars—on a political basis.

The future costs of the present social-security system are subject to wild guesses running from $200 to $500 billion over the next fifteen or twenty years.

Incomes never can keep pace with the rising level of prices. If inflation is not stopped, Social Security is a fraud. As the number of retired workers grows, they should enlist in the cause of sound money. Honest

---

3 Charlotte Towle, *Common Human Needs: An Interpretation for Staff in Public Assistance Agencies*, Department of Health, Education and Welfare, Social Security Administration, Washington, D.C., 1945, p. 57.

pensions require an honest dollar, a dollar that will buy in the future what is promised today.

Noting humanity's eternal hope for security, the Reverend Samuel M. Shoemaker says that the politicians' promises win converts and votes. His summarization: ". . . the longing of the Godless for some kind of protection. When we lose God we turn to what looks like the next most powerful thing, which is the state."[4]

That political "benefits" can lead to slavery is the greatest lesson of history. The philosopher and historian Plutarch said, in 100 A.D.:

> There is no doubt that the real destroyer of the liberties of any people is he who spreads among them bounties and largess.[5]

President Wilson declared:

> . . . I don't want to live under a philanthropy. I don't want to be taken care of by the government, directly or by any instruments through which the government is acting. I want to have right and justice prevail. So far as I am concerned give me the right and justice and I'll undertake to take care of myself.[6]

> I will not live under trustees if I can help it. No group of men less than the majority has a right to tell me how I have got to live in America. I will submit to the majority, because I have been trained to do it—though I may sometimes have my private opinion even of the majority. I do not care how wise, how patriotic, the trustees may be, I have never heard of any group of men in whose hands I am willing to lodge the liberties of America in trust.[7]

---

4 Samuel M. Shoemaker, Letter to Mrs. Robert Cruise McManus, August 29, 1962.
5 Dryden-Clough (trans.), *Plutarch's Lives* (Modern Library, New York, 1932), p. 271.
6 Woodrow Wilson, Address at Pueblo, Colorado, October 7, 1912, quoted by John Wells Davidson (ed.), *Crossroads of Freedom: The 1912 Campaign Speeches of Woodrow Wilson*, (Yale University Press, New Haven, Connecticut, 1956), pp. 356-7.
7 Woodrow Wilson, "Freemen Need No Guardian," *Fortnightly Review*, February, 1913, Vol. 99, pp. 209-218, reprinted in Woodrow Wilson, *The New Democracy:*

James F. Byrnes, former governor of South Carolina, former senator, Supreme Court justice, and secretary of state, has said:

> The spirit of self-reliance that animated the early settlers and for more than a century inspired our people to exercise their initiative and develop this country, while preserving their independence, is unfortunately departing from the people.[8]

The passion for security is a fatal sickness when it becomes more important for an individual than confidence and self-respect. The greater danger to the nation is that the coming generation of young people may believe that dependence on government is a way of life.

The experiment in collectivism may have become a permanent part of our economic and social life. It adheres to the collectivist principle of legal forces and penalties to make the individual conform. So far as possible, its management should be kept within the bounds of the American tradition of liberty and justice for all.

Individual self-reliance in the United States developed the strongest economy the world has ever known. Because this great economic strength can be quickly converted into military strength, we have also enjoyed political security.

Compared to this strength, the welfare state, with its pretended security, is a crutch on which civilizations ancient and modern have hobbled to their graves.

One thing can be said with assurance. If the American people can maintain their free economy and cast off the chains that have been placed on it in two decades of seduction by the welfare state, their strength will be "as the strength of ten." It is the might of right, and they can walk securely and fearlessly in the world, even in a world overcast by a great Communist empire.

Presidential Messages, Addresses and Other Papers (1913-1917), (Harper & Bros., New York, 1926), Vol. I, p. 12.
8 James F. Byrnes, Speech at the Conference of Southern Governors in Biloxi, Mississippi, November 21, 1949.

Chapter Eleven
THE THEORY OF COMMUNISM

American Experiments

COMMUNISM in the United States is older than the country itself. Public or collective ownership of all property—the basic economic theory of communism—was established by the first colonists from Europe 350 years ago. Since then, more than 200 communities have been founded on that principle, survived briefly, and disbanded.

The first permanent English settlement was at Jamestown, Virginia, in 1607. Settlers were promised security under a planned economy. The London Company's charter from the king forbade private ownership of land. Industry and agriculture were community activities, and the community had a monopoly on labor and its products. It was a miniature of today's Communist countries.

The colonists practiced a communism much nearer to theoretical communism than is today's Russian variety. To each man was allotted his share of the work. All production went into a common warehouse, from which the requirements of each were portioned out.

Of Jamestown, the historian Edward Eggleston wrote: "To escape from the anarchy which resulted from a system that sank the interest of an individual in that of the community, it had been needful to arm De la Warr with the sharp sword of martial law."[1] Governors De la Warr and Dale were tyrants, but communism required tyrannical measures, without

---

[1] Edward Eggleston, *The Beginners of A Nation* (D. Appleton & Co., New York, 1896), p. 42.

which the colony would have perished. The governors could condemn to death any who refused to obey their orders.

The planned farming included oranges, lemons, and other tropical fruits that have not grown in the climate since those early days. An iron foundry, glass works, soap factory, and other industries were shipped from England. Recruits were promised a six-hour work day, with a house, food, and clothing supplied by the community.

Planners in London ran the colony by remote control. Four-fifths of the colonists died of hunger, exposure, or epidemics. Governors who dictated every detail of the colonists' lives reported malingering, lost boats, desertion, murder, and cannibalism; nearly everyone pretended to be too sick or "too weak" to work. "They would eat their fish raw rather than they would go a stone's throw to fetch wood and dresse it." A stern martinet with Communist efficiency tortured men by "breaking on the wheel" for not obeying, and split the ears or ran bodkins through the tongues of any who complained. Even convicts refused to go to the new Utopia after reports of conditions reached England.

A petition which a few brave colonists sent to the king across the ocean is so expressive of the despair of all oppressed people that it deserves a place in history: "Rather than be reduced to live under the like government, we desire his majesty that commissioners be sent over to hang us."

Colonists as well as the London Company, which had expected handsome profits, realized that the communal system was a failure. In 1616, each settler was given three acres of land, later increased to fifty, to farm as he pleased. Individual incentive and competition came to the colony. Virginia has prospered ever since.

Captain John Smith wrote of his vast experience in the budding Old Dominion of those bygone years:

> ... when our people were fed out of the common store, and labored jointly in the manuring of the ground, and planting corn, glad was that man that could slip from his labor; nay, the most honest of them in a general business would not take so much faithful and true pains in a week, as now he will doe in a day; neither cared they for the increase, presuming that howsoever their harvest prospered the

general store must maintain them. By which means we reaped not so much corn from the labor of thirty men as three men have done for themselves.[2]

Though religious beliefs united each New England colony, the trial of collectivism was as bitter as in Virginia. The Pilgrims landed from the *Mayflower* in 1620 and established the Plymouth Colony. The Puritans came to Salem, not far distant in these days, and the Massachusetts Bay Colony, started in 1628 with some thousand colonists, was the largest in the New World. Both settlements followed the famous dictum: "Those who work not, shall not eat," and famine quickly followed.

Three years of misery were enough to show the Plymouth Colony that the Communist pattern brought neither freedom nor a decent living. In 1632, the land and property were divided among the families. The Massachusetts Bay Colony did not learn from the sad experience of others.

Governor William Bradford of Plymouth summarized the change from a planned economy and government ownership to private initiative. His old-style English is as pertinent today as 300 years ago. He wrote:

> This [private ownership] had a very good success; for it made all hands very industrious, so as much more corn was planted than other-wise would have been by any means the Governor or any other could use, and saved him a good deal of trouble and gave far better contents.
>
> The women now went willingly into the field, and took their little-ones with them to set corn, which before would aledg weakness, and inabilitie; whom to have compelled would have been thought great tiranie and oppression.
>
> The experience that was had in this common course and condition, tried sundrie years, and that amongst godly and sober men, may well evince the vanitie of that conceite of Platos and other ancients,

---

2 Captain John Smith in "An account given by Ralph Hamor, Secretary of the Colony in 1611," quoted by Conway Whittle Sams, *The Conquest of Virginia, The Third Attempt* (G. P. Putnam's Sons, New York, 1939), p. 155.

applauded by some of later times;—*that the taking away of property, and bringing in communitie into a common wealth, would make them happy and flourishing; as if they were wiser than God.* For this communitie (so far as it was) was found to breed much confusion and discontent, and retard much imployment that would have been to their benefit and comfort.

For the young-men that were most able and fitte for labor and service did repine that they should spend their time and strength to worke for any other man's wives and children, without any recompense. The strong, or man of parts, had no more in divission of victails and cloaths, than he that was weak and not able to doe a quarter the other could; this was thought injuestice; . . .

And for men's wives to be commanded to doe service for other men, as dressing their meats, washing their cloaths, etc . . . , they deemed it a kind of slaverie, neither could many husbands well brooke it.[3]

[author's italics]

Hundreds of communal settlements have been attempted in the United States. Except for a few, they have disappeared and are forgotten.

Ephrata was founded in 1732, a hundred years after the colonial failures, by German emigrants near Lancaster, Pennsylvania. It had flour, lumber, paper, and flaxseed mills, workshops, and a communal commissary. In 1798 it disbanded, but The Cloisters still stand as evidence that the pioneers' handiwork was more durable than their theories. Industrious Ephrata thrives today under private ownership.

Brook Farm, near West Roxbury, Massachusetts, led a short and glamorous life from 1841 to 1846. It had two hundred acres of land and a few calloused palms. Emerson, Hawthorne, and other writers, artists, and enthusiasts lived there. All shared in the work, but it was a disappointing failure.

---

3 William Bradford, *History of the Plymouth Plantation*, Charles Dean (ed.), (Little, Brown & Co., Boston, 1856), pp. 134-5.

Oneida, New York, was started in 1846 with 300 co-religionists and 650 fertile acres. All property was held in common, and "mutual criticism" replaced written laws. The younger generation straggled away to localities with a little more law and more individual freedom. In 1881 it was reorganized as a joint stock company.

When the community at Amana, Iowa, was launched in 1855, all land and industries were owned by the church and run by the elders. They provided social security, education, medical care, and other physical needs. The financial strain increased until capitalistic profits and wages were introduced in 1932. Prosperity returned.

King Ben and Queen Mary Purnell founded the House of David in St. Joseph, Michigan. After King Ben's death in 1927, the property was divided into two portions, and Queen Mary and her followers named their community the City of David. Both groups are industrious, operating the largest motel in Michigan, greenhouses, hotel, amusement park, a bearded baseball team, workshops, and restaurants. No meats are served, but the variety of drinks is extensive. Barbers are banned. When Queen Mary died at the age of 90 in 1953, her grandchildren sued for property around $75,000. Her followers replied that individual ownership was contrary to her religion and that everything belonged to the community.

A community may live in harmony, voluntary or forced, but rivalry for power and property often becomes as keen as in any free competitive society.

Individuals in this country are free to pool their resources and hold all property and production in common as long as they obey local and state laws. Members of the few such communities that exist today are united by social or religious convictions, and the matter of property ownership is only incidental. They emphatically deny being Communistic.

The old adage, "The laborer is worthy of his hire," has been true through the ages. Until the world becomes a Utopia where all can live without work, the lack of profit incentive will be a fatal defect of communism. When men are driven to work like animals, their services are worth little more than those of animals.

Communism was tried and abandoned in America. Though many of its principles are long discarded even in the Soviet Union, that country gives it lip service and tries to force it on the world. Its advocates, naïvely sincere or greedy for power, extol it as the only salvation for a better life. In essence, it is coercive total collectivism of the economy, politics, and culture of the people.

Economic collectivism is socialism, the political and economic theory of social organization based on governmental ownership and management of the essential means of production and distribution of goods—land, mineral resources, basic industries, railroads, public utilities.

Although socialism pretends to confine itself to economic collectivism, it assumes full control of education and propaganda. It aims toward the destruction of religion, the spread of atheism, and complete control of the social and cultural lives of all. It calls for the complete abolition of all private property. In its fullest expression, it is communism.

Dialectical Materialism

It is a mistake to underestimate the hold that communism has on the minds of millions. To understand its appeal we have to study the Communist ideology.

"Marxian dialectics" is the basis. "Dialectics," from a Greek word meaning "to speak" or a "dialog," for centuries was regarded as a synonym for logic.

Marxian dialectics is based upon the idea, elaborated by the German philosopher Friedrich Hegel, that truth and reality are not simple things but are matters of opposites (thesis and antithesis) which, when synthesized, produce a whole actuality (synthesis).

With Marxian dialectics you can "comprehend" with certainty that the thesis (capitalism) creates its antithesis (the working class) and out of the clash of the two must come the synthesis (the Communist Utopia).

Hegel accepted the truth of the existence of the spirit of the universe, without which all is without meaning. Marx and Engels discarded the spirit and made Communist theory strictly materialistic, presenting their doctrine as "dialectical materialism" or "dimat."

Dimat presents the simple proposition that, since man is the product of matter and the laws of nature, and not the handiwork of a nonexistent spiritual Being, then Communistic materialism is a much better solution to mankind's problems than any solution based upon the spiritual concept of human origin.

Dimat is altogether pragmatic—it has no moral sense of direction. It does not hesitate to adopt morally evil means to a desired end. Slavery, mass murder, genocide are acceptable for desired ends. Wrote Lenin, "For the Communist morality consists entirely of a compact united discipline . . ."[4]

Marx and Engels feared the tendency of government to become tyrannical, and Marx assured his followers that with dimat, once the proletariat reached power the government would wither away. Engels prophesied, in his *Origin of the Family, Private Property and the State*:

The society that will organize production on the basis of free and equal association of the producers will put the whole machinery of state where it will then belong; into the museum of antiquities, side by side of the spinning wheel and the bronze axe.[5]

In the Communist Manifesto, Marx and Engels predicted that the unceasing improvement of machinery would make the livelihood of the workers ever more precarious and their standard of living inevitably lower. We now see, however, that the welfare of the workers has risen in direct proportion to the capital investment in tools.

So it seems that the law of Reverse Results applies to that intellectual gandy-dance, dialectic materialism.

Lenin described dialectical materialism as having "flexibility of conception, flexibility to the point of the identity of opposites—that is the essence of the dialectic."

But this is the "flexibility" of the insane.

---

4 V. I. Lenin, "Address to the Young Communist League," quoted by Committee on Foreign Affairs, Sub-Committee No. 5, National and International Movements, "House Document No. 619," *The Strategy and Tactics of World Communism*, Supplement I, *One Hundred Years of Communism 1848-1948* (U.S. Government Printing Office, Washington, D.C., 1948), p. 73.

5 Friederich Engels, "The Origin of the Family, Private Property and the State," quoted in *Marx and Engels Selected Works* (Foreign Languages Publishing House, Moscow, 1955), Vol. II, p. 321.

Chapter Twelve
ALTERNATIVE TO SOCIALISM

UNDER our free economy, workers dissatisfied with management have an excellent opportunity to correct conditions without socialism. It is simply to buy control of the corporations.

Workers have done this in several plywood factories in the West. At the start they paid much higher wages than did the orthodox corporations, but they soon found that the part of a sales dollar that could be paid in wages was about the same in their case as in the others. Worn-out and obsolete machinery had to be replaced. An efficient sales force was necessary, as the market for plywood was competitive. Factory problems were no different.

Then the workers were confronted with a problem of owners. Workers who reached the age of retirement, feeling that they had a capital interest, wished to leave their savings invested there. Others wanted to will stock to their heirs. Sale of stock to private investors also was possible. To prevent this, most worker-owned corporations had a stock provision that barred anyone that was not a worker in the particular enterprise from owning stock, or specified that a new purchaser must be approved by a factory committee, or limited the number of shares that one worker might own.

One cooperative required every applicant for a job to purchase one share of stock for $2500 before being employed and to purchase one more share after he got the job. He paid for the second share in installments. No worker was allowed more than two shares. This concern began with $750,000 paid-in capital. It is reported that the workers in this plant produced from 10% to 20% more than they had done under one owner.

A recent editorial in *The New York Times* comments on the take-over of a hat company by a union:

JOEL R. BELKNAP

The United Hatters, Cap and Millinery Workers Union has taken a step that confounds commonly accepted ideas about labor's place in the economic scheme of things. The union has bought a controlling interest in the Merrimac Hat Corporation of Amesbury, Mass., whose employees are all union members, and has appointed its own officers to six of the nine places on the company's board of directors. The president and other administrative officers will be retained by the new owner.

The more one thinks about this the more bewildering the implications become. In the first place there is the question of who is boss around there. Certainly the management is, but the employees will control the management. And what becomes of the theory that there is a conflict of interest in a capitalist system between capital and labor when they are one and the same? Karl Marx must be turning in his grave.

Somehow, though, the whole situation may work out to everyone's advantage. If the union hadn't come to the rescue the biggest plant in little Amesbury would have folded up and its 325 employees would have lost their jobs. There would have been no more dividends for the stockholders, who include outside investors.

Of course there's the risk that the new owners won't make a go of it. But in 1954 the same union made a $200,000 loan to a hat company to keep the business alive, and many of the union's members also made advances. That company has now paid all the members' loans and all but $25,000 of what the union lent—and the employees got a wage increase.

Anyway, all this is a "people's capitalism" with a vengeance. Soviet papers please note.[1]

Union leaders, all of whom have graduated from the status of workers to big businessmen, are well aware of the opportunities of ownership. They also know its responsibilities and risks. Some union members with a high

---

1 *The New York Times*, January 26, 1959.

sense of cooperation have shared losses with their employers when the businesses got into financial trouble.

Using its retirement fund alone, the United Mine Workers of America could, in a few years, take over control of all the large coal companies in the country. If coal companies are making large profits, as John L. Lewis often asserted, why are they not good investments? The miners are in a position to supervise the management closely and to know the industry's every detail of trade and finance.

It is possible to get into the coal business in West Virginia with an investment of only a few hundred dollars. If any group of workers think the price of meat is too high, a meat packing plant can be purchased for much less than the cost of building a new one.

The Electrical Workers Union owns and operates through a special corporation a 556-unit luxury apartment building. And the Bricklayers Union owns a commercial office building.

In Cleveland, the Brotherhood of Locomotive Engineers owns two big Cleveland office buildings and an apartment hotel. The union also operates a life and accident insurance company. In St. Louis, the Optical Worker's Union runs a wholesale optical company.

Karl Marx saw one side of the worker-owner relationship and never opened his eyes to the risks and responsibilities on the other side. If workers are exploited by industry, as he said, by underpayment of wages and overpricing of manufactured goods, the free economy of the United States gives a wonderful opportunity for change. Why did not Marx, as Henry Ford did later, start a small industry, treat the workers better, and sell their products more cheaply? Many thousands of concerns in the United States have demonstrated that no more capital than that required to open a blacksmith shop is necessary for a beginning. Today, unions are not limited to pioneering with small businesses. Many have enough millions to buy into the biggest and oldest going concerns.

Automobile agencies and summer resorts are among union ventures. The Teamsters' Union invested a million dollars in Montgomery Ward stock during a proxy fight a few years ago. The Auto Workers' Union advanced $300,000 to an automobile company to enlarge its sales force and bought enough stock in another company to prevent a competitor from getting control. An independent union saved a big Philadelphia store from going out of business.

Such stock holdings naturally strengthen a union's bargaining position. The National Labor Relations Board has ruled that a union owning or controlling a corporation can negotiate with a competitor and even strike or picket the rival. Another ruling held that a union owning a building can compel its tenants to hire only union members.

Being both wage owner and stockholder may put a union on the horns of a dilemma. Labor demands for higher wages can reduce dividends and stock values. Some leaders shun the dual role, but the Potters' Union plays the market profitably, and the Central Labor Union in Philadelphia employs a securities counselor to advise on stock investments.

Outside business as a union sideline is not always a bonanza. The typographical union started newspapers in several cities where it was having labor disputes. Members soon protested that the newspapers were not helping the union cause and that their steady losses were a serious drain on the treasury, and they were sold to other publishers.

Worker-owned plants can be the strongest kind of competition. Some labor unions, however, are opposed to worker-owned plants. The reasons are clear. In a worker-owned plant, every worker is also employer and owner, and no individual who is not a worker on the plant's payroll can be an owner or stockholder. Consequently, when wages, dividends, or any of the unending problems of the business are threshed out, only the employer-workers of the plants are interested. No union is involved, and union membership has only a social or sentimental value.

Political worker "ownership" has reached its inevitable outcome in the Soviet Union. The government owns all physical property, and the Communist Party dictates the activities of all organizations, including trade unions and government. The worker is considered to be the owner of the factory on the theory that he owns the government. But because he is only one among 200,000,000 theoretical owners, he does not have a right to whisper about wages, working conditions, or other problems of his own factory.

When the new Soviet government took over factories and business and threw out the former owners, officials were dedicated to Marx's untried dogmas of communism. Every factory was turned over to its delegated worker-owners. The workers, each having one vote, elected shop committees and the top factory committee to run the establishment. As much time was given to meetings as to work. Naturally, the unskilled laborers, or "black workers," exalted by Communist doctrine, were in the majority and elected executives from their own ranks. It was soon evident that a spellbinder was rarely an efficient manager.

Even in our country, with all its freedoms, genuine worker-owned plants have their difficulties. Management is unwieldy and some plants have been obliged to close down while the worker-owners argued problems and made decisions. Some worker-owners want all the profits paid in dividends and have little concern for reserves for contingencies and obsolescence. In a majority of cases the worker-owners elect a board of directors, who in turn hire a general manager.

Competitors are pressuring Congress to withdraw the special tax exemptions enjoyed by all worker-owned cooperatives, especially farmer cooperatives. Farmer cooperatives, however, are not true worker-owner enterprises; they hire employees as do other merchandising establishments. In some of them, ownership of stock in the corporation, which is the owner and employer, is not limited to working farmers. Their lower taxes enable them to undersell regular corporations, and they are growing fast, with annual sales in the billions. It appears that the government, to protect its own great income derived from corporation taxes, will be forced to end the tax "saving" of the cooperatives.

Between the extremes of worker-ownership and individual or corporate ownership are profit-sharing companies. On the fringes are the numerous companies which distribute an annual bonus to employees. All are forms of worker participation, or profit sharing, differing in structure and operation.

In one factory a bonus may be part of an employment contract. In another there may be a voluntary award by management to employees based on earnings of the year just ended. It compares to an extra dividend for stockholders. In general, a bonus fund is divided among top executives and such employees as qualify by wage scales and length of employment.

Profit sharing is more formal and comprehensive. The percentage and distribution is fixed as definitely as any wage scale. Qualifications for eligibility are equally definite.

Profit-sharing agreements between employers and employees are increasing in number. Procter and Gamble, the Endicott Shoe Company, Hormel Meat Packers, and the Eastman Kodak Company have shared profits with their employees for years. The system becomes a cushion against losses and layoffs. Wages are tied to the firm's income and go up or down accordingly. With profit sharing, workers and employers profit or economize together.

Another form of employer-employee relations is being worked out in West Germany. Known as *Mitbestimmungrecht*, or right of joint management, it gives the unions a direct voice in the management of a firm. The German Trade Union, by threatening in 1951 to strike, obtained the right of joint management in the iron, coal, and steel industries. The contract provides that five members of the board of directors of every company shall be elected by the trade unions and five directors by management, with a neutral chairman. Still more powerful bodies, "senates" with similar representation and with power to control the entire industry, are set up.

The Communist state of Yugoslavia also has announced experiments in worker management of factories. They choose a council, which then selects a smaller board of directors. This board is empowered to confer with the state manager of the plant on such management problems as contracts, wage rates, discipline, promotion, and dismissal.

Whatever the country, evidence accumulates that the system that offers the greatest freedom in making direct, man-to-man relations between management and labor possible, and the simplest and clearest relation between effort and reward, will prosper.

Benjamin F. Fairless, former president of the United States Steel Corporation, once figured out that if each worker had 87 shares of the company's stock, the workers would own the corporation. At the market quotation he used, each also would have 7% income on his investment. Mr. Fairless said:

> By investing $10 a week apiece—which is about what our steel workers gained in a recent wage increase—the employees of U.S. Steel could buy

all of the outstanding common stock in less than seven years; and—except for the relatively small fixed sum that is paid in dividends on the preferred stock—our employees would then be entitled to receive all of those so-called "bloated profits" they have heard so much about. But here, I'm afraid, they would be in for a disappointing surprise. At current rates, the total dividend on 87 shares is only $261 a year.

But in order to control U.S. Steel, these employees would not even have to purchase 87 shares apiece. Sixty-two shares of common stock would give them a voting majority. . . . Then they could elect their own Board of Directors, fire the present management, put Phil Murray in my job and run the business to suit themselves.[2]

Karl Marx maintained that machines would enslave men; he never imagined that the time would come when workers could own the machines they operate if they cared to do so.

---

2 Benjamin F. Fairless, *The Great Mistake of Karl Marx*, Address at Thirty-Fifth Annual Meeting of the Pennsylvania State Chamber of Commerce, Pittsburgh, October 22, 1952 (U.S. Steel Corp., New York), pp. 9-10.

Chapter Thirteen
MORALITY AND GOVERNMENT

Our Unparalleled productivity and standard of living are not the consequences solely of the economic system. The economic system is, itself, the result of our ethical and moral concepts, of our faith in the divine right and dignity of the individual.

The Founders forbade the establishment of a state religion. Our people are free to choose any religion they wish, or none. But the majority of people believe, as did our Founders, that religion, morality, and knowledge are necessary to good government; that unless we are governed by God we will be governed by tyrants; that religion and morality are the indispensable supports to all habits that lead to economic and political prosperity. George Washington said:

> Reason and experience forbid us to expect that natural morality can prevail in the exclusion of religious right; true religion affords government its surest support.[1]

Statesmen and economists agree that, *without honor*, little is left of any economic or social system. The universal law of cause and effect makes this so. Morality cannot be compromised, not even by the use of evil to obtain good ends.

When Alexis de Tocqueville visited this country a hundred years ago, he wrote:

---

[1] *The Writings of George Washington from the Original Manuscript Sources* (U.S. Government Printing Office, Washington, D.C., 1940), Vol. 35, p. 229.

THE STORY OF FREE ENTERPRISE

I sought for the greatness and genius of America in her commodious harbors and her ample rivers, and it was not there; in her fertile fields and boundless prairies and it was not there. Not until I went to the churches of America and heard her pulpits aflame with righteousness did I understand the secret of her genius and power. America is great because she is good and if America ever ceases to be good America will cease to be great.[2]

Theodore Roosevelt said:

... Freedom thus conceived is a constructive force, which enables an intelligent and good man to do better things than he could do without it; which is in its essence the substitution of self-restraint for external restraint—the substitution of a form of restraint which promotes progress for the form which retards it.[3]

The world-famous scientist, Dr. Charles P. Steinmetz has this to say about spiritual force:

Here is a force which history clearly teaches has been the greatest power in the development of men. ... Yet we have merely been playing with it and have never seriously studied it as we have the physical forces. Some day people will learn that material things do not bring happiness, and are of little use in making men and women creative and powerful. Then the scientists of the world will turn their laboratories over to the study of prayer, and the spiritual forces which as yet have hardly been scratched.[4]

---

[2] Quoted by Dwight D. Eisenhower in Address at the New England "Forward to '54" Dinner, Boston, Massachusetts, September 21, 1953.
[3] Theodore Roosevelt, Speech at Gettysburg, Pennsylvania, May 30, 1904 in *Collected Works*, National Edition, Vol. XI, p. 326.
[4] Charles P. Steinmetz quoted by Roger Babson, "The Meaning of Religious Education to our American Life," *The Christian Advocate*, California Edition, September 11, 1930, p. 10.

Every problem discussed in this book reduces to a moral issue. We believe that every man is born with certain natural, unalienable rights, rights that no other men have the right to take away. A government—our own or another—that does so commits a wrong. This is the basis of the philosophy of free economic enterprise.

Personal freedom is the most important of the unalienable rights. Socialism and communism are basically wrong because they abolish personal freedom. Personal economic freedom cannot exist without a free economic system which makes a free market.

Because the free market is the fairest of all markets for all concerned, it is morally wrong to interfere with the operations of the free market except to maintain order and justice therein. Arbitrary intereference means that someone is treated unfairly—in short, is plundered.

"The short triumph of Athenian liberty," asserted Lord Acton, "and its quick decline, belong to an age which possessed no fixed standards of right and wrong."[5]

In our study of booms and depressions we saw that credit—a factor of both—is based upon confidence and that inflation is thoroughly immoral credit manipulation or legalized counterfeiting. It destroys faith and the financial structure that rests upon faith. In modern monetary systems, inflation operates mainly through expansion of credit. When distrust appears, it spreads like wildfire through the credit structure; inflation has the seeds of its own destruction. Governments are powerless to do much about a depression once it has begun—governments themselves are the chief target of distrust.

The high efficiency of our economy exists mainly because of its integrity. Honor in business is an absolute necessity. The liar is the most troublesome but also the most inefficient and destructive factor in industry.

Confidence in the spoken word is one reason for the high efficiency of American business. Our quickest means of communication is the telephone, and very few conversations are recorded. Although we follow up with written confirmations, the greater part of American business is

---

5 John Emerich Edward Dalberg-Acton, *The History of Freedom and Other Essays* (Macmillan & Co., Ltd., London, 1909), p. 70.

transacted by telephone. Oral contracts involving millions of dollars are transacted every day.

Eric Rogers, when president of the Arkansas Free Enterprise Association, stated:

> It is not true, as some people seem to believe, that graft, petty or otherwise, and various kinds of dishonesty must inevitably be a part of all human undertakings. As the same executive pointed out "high moral standards do exist and must exist to make possible the efficient production and distribution of $325 billion worth of goods and services in this country every year!" Fraud and commercial bribery are almost nonexistent here, and millions of transactions, some involving large sums, are completed every year without written contracts or formal guarantees. On the stock exchanges, billions of dollars' worth of property are bought and sold by a word or a sign, and the agreements are invariably honored. This executive said that his own company has credit bills amounting to about $900 million a year to over a million different individuals and concerns, yet the bad debt loss over the past five years has averaged 1/50 of one percent.[6]

In the consulting engineering business you have an office in which is a desk, a drafting board, a few drawing instruments and some books—total value, a few hundred dollars. But if you have a reputation for ability and integrity, you are rich. Ability alone is not worth much. Without a good name you are poor.

Paul A. Redmond, president of the Southern States Industrial Council, says:

> In any business there is an intangible asset we call "goodwill." It is something you cannot touch but it is always the determining factor between success and failure. It is the composite of many elements, but basically it

---

6 Eric Rogers, "Morality in Our National Life," *The Free Enterpriser* (Arkansas Free Enterprise Association, Little Rock, Arkansas), February, 1952, p. 3.

results from the production of an honest article sold at a fair price creating confidence in the mind of the buying public.⁷

Engineers will assure you that "the spirit of the living creature is in the wheels." The quality of machinery is an expression of the quality of the men who made it. The model T Ford car expressed the personality of Henry Ford. It was reliable, tenacious, ingenious, and dependable; irritating in some details, but good value for the money.

The Founders of our country believed emphatically in honor and morality.

George Washington said, in his Farewell Address:

> Of all the dispositions and habits that lead to political prosperity, religion and morality are indispensable supports.... Where is the security for property, for reputation, for life, if the sense of religious obligations desert the oaths which are the instruments of investigation in courts of justice?⁸

An immoral people is incapable of self-government, because any government it may set up will legalize plundering and soon must collapse. It will be plagued with deficit financing, inflation, subsidies that destroy, controls that strangle, irredeemable currency and confiscatory taxation—all fatal to economic growth and stability.

Willam Penn was convinced that unless we are governed by God we will be governed by tyrants.

The Declaration of Independence emphasizes the laws of nature and nature's God, and it concludes with these words: "We mutually pledge to each other our lives, our fortunes and our sacred honor." Thomas Jefferson stood for "equal and exact justice to all men" and warned again and again against corruption in government.

---

7 Paul A. Redmond, Letter to Joel R. Belknap, November 27, 1953.
8 *The Writings of George Washington*, Vol. 35, p. 229.

THE STORY OF FREE ENTERPRISE

The Founders believed that morality, industry, and self-control formulate the laws that bring prosperity to men and nations. Without them, economic improvement brings on luxury, vice, and corruption.

F. A. Harper says in *Morals & The Welfare State:*

> Economics and morals are both parts of one inseparable body of truth. They must, therefore, be in harmony with one another. What is right morally must also be right economically, and vice versa. Since morals are a guide to betterment and to self-protection, economic policies that violate Moral Truth, will, with certainty, cause degeneration and self-destruction.[9]

A horrifying contrast to the Founders' principles of honesty and decency between men is Lenin's summary of the code of communism:

> We say that our morality is entirely subordinated to the interest of the class struggle of the proletariat. . . .[10]

> For the Communist, morality consists entirely of compact united discipline and conscious mass struggle against the exploiters. We do not believe in eternal morality, and we expose all the fables about morality. . . .[11]

> And so, down with religion and long live atheism! The dissemination of atheist views is our chief task. . . .[12]

Earl Browder, when he was the head of the Communist Party in this country, quoted from that guide to dishonesty, the Communist Manifesto, as follows:

---

9 F. A. Harper, *Morals and the Welfare State* (Foundation for Economic Education, Irvington-on-Hudson, New York), p. 4.
10 V. I. Lenin, quoted by Committee on Foreign Affairs, Sub-Committee No. 5, National and International Movements, "House Document No. 619," *The Strategy and Tactics of World Communism*, Supplement I, *One Hundred Years of Communism 1848-1948* (U.S. Government Printing Office, Washington, D.C., 1948), p. 71.
11 *Ibid., p.* 73.
12 *Ibid.,* p. 71.

... Law, morality, religion, are to him [the Communist] so many bourgeois prejudices, behind which lurk in ambush just as many bourgeois interest.[13]

The Congress of 1787 passed the Northwest Ordinance before the Constitution was adopted. It said:

"Religion, morality and knowledge being necessary to good government and the happiness of mankind, schools as a means of education shall forever be encouraged."[14]

An autocratic government with the moral standards of the Communists cannot be trusted to keep faith with its own people or to observe its treaties. Its organized power, constantly poised to accomplish our downfall, means that there can be no security for the free governments of the world except in armaments.

Through the years, countless Americans have reaffirmed the principle that truth and honesty between men and between nations is the only sure foundation of a secure and happy society.

Former President Hoover has warned:

Our greatest danger is not from invasion by foreign armies. Our dangers are that we may commit suicide from within . . . by cynical acceptance of dishonor.[15]

Herbert Agar, the social and political historian, says:

Every civilization rests on a set of promises. . . . If the promises are broken too often, the civilization dies, no matter how rich it may be, or how

---

13 Earl Browder, *Ibid.*, p. 12.
14 *Northwest Ordinance*, quoted by Charles A. Beard and Mary R. Beard, *The Rise of American Civilization* (The Macmillan Co., New York, 1935), Vol. I, pp. 531-2.
15 Herbert Hoover, *Addresses Upon the American Road: 1950-1955* (Stanford University Press, Stanford, California, 1955), p. 117.

mechanically clever. Hope and faith depend on the promises; if hope and faith go, everything goes.[16]

And the historian and economist Friedrich A. Hayek writes:

> Freedom to order our own conduct in the sphere where material circumstances force a choice upon us, and responsibility for the arrangement of our own life according to our own conscience, is the air in which alone moral sense grows and in which moral values are daily re-created in the free decision of the individual. Responsibility not to a superior, but to one's conscience, the awareness of a duty not exacted by compulsion, the necessity to decide which of the things one values are to be sacrificed to others, and bear the consequences of one's own decision, are the very essence of any morals which deserves the name.[17]

The main issue is joined. We believe we are working nearer to what is right. A free economic and social system continually purges itself of wrong, because of the inherent competitive superiority of right over wrong. Communist literature denies that morality has any permanent or absolute principles and insists that right is entirely relative to human experience. This is pragmatism.

Pragmatism is a philosophical belief founded by Ferdinand C. S. Schiller and William James. Through the medium of John Dewey, it has profoundly affected theological and educational theories. It is a "philosophy of experience." In essence it maintains that there are no absolute values of truth or of right and wrong. An idea is "true" if it works in practice. What is right and good is that which serves to achieve "life adjustment" by experience or "free activity." Nothing is evil if "good" ends are achieved.

---

16 Herbert Agar, *Forbes Magazine of Business and Finance*, September 1, 1960, p. 58.
17 Friederich A. Hayek, *The Road to Serfdom* (The University of Chicago Press, 1944), p. 212.

By this philosophy, nothing that happened in the life of Josef Stalin proved him wrong; his life was a huge success. The associates he treacherously assassinated, the millions he murdered all served for an "adjustment to society." Stalin's experience with banditry was very "successful" in so far as he escaped punishment. His "success" has resulted in slavery for hundreds of millions of people, however.

Conscience, like a compass, may swing wildly for a time, but this truly divine censor finally points to the right. It points to principle over experience, although human experience always confirms moral principles.

And in his Farewell Address, George Washington paid his respects to collective morals:

> The common and continual mischiefs of the spirit of party are sufficient to make it the interest and duty of a wise people to discourage and restrain it. It serves always to distract the public councils, and enfeeble the public administration.[18]

You will see persons whom you personally know to be frank and honest take positions in city, county, state, or federal government, only to condone and even assist in undertakings which they know perfectly well are wrong. "Power corrupts," observed Lord Acton, and it seems as if the greater the power the greater the corruption.

The ability and morality of any collective group tends to become that of the lowest common denominator. The common denominator may be high, however, as was the case with the Constitutional Convention. It has been said that never before had so much wisdom from so many men of real greatness been applied so successfully to a difficult task. The lofty tone of the final draft was mainly due to the efforts of two men, Benjamin Franklin and George Washington.

The delegates had wrangled for many weeks and had not agreed upon a single word of the Constitution. Franklin arose and addressed Washington, who was in the chair:

---

18 *Writings of George Washington*, Vol. 35, p. 227.

THE STORY OF FREE ENTERPRISE

> Mr. President, the slow progress we have made after weeks of close attendance and continued reasoning with each other, with different sentiments on almost every question . . . is, methinks, a melancholy proof of the imperfection of human understanding. . . . We have been assured, sir, in the Sacred Writings that "Except the Lord build the house, they labor in vain that build it. . . . I therefore beg leave to move that our deliberations be held in the Assembly every morning before we proceed to business.[19]

From that moment the assembly made progress. On September 15, 1787, the draft was completed, but voices were raised against it. Unless you write into this Constitution some popular fallacies to fool and please the people, they will not adopt it, ran the argument.

Washington arose and said:

> It is too probable that no plan we propose will be adopted. Perhaps another dreadful conflict is to be sustained. . . . If, to please the people, we offer what we ourselves disapprove, how can we afterwards defend our work? Let us raise a standard to which the wise and honest can repair. The event is in the hands of God.[20]

Later, William Pitt was to say of the Constitution:

> It will be the wonder and admiration of all future generations and the model of all future Constitutions.[21]

William E. Gladstone, prime minister of Britain, on September 18, 1878, rendered his opinion:

---

19 Benjamin Franklin, quoted by Saul K. Padover, *The World of the Founding Fathers* (Thomas Yoseloff, New York, 1960), p. 170.
20 George Washington quoted by Gouverneur Morris, quoted by Carl Van Doren, *The Great Rehearsal* (The Viking Press, New York, 1948), p. 15.
21 William Pitt, quoted by Joseph Dilway Sawyer, *Washington* (The Macmillan Co., New York, 1927), Vol. 2, p. 139.

> The American Constitution is, so far as I can see, the most wonderful work ever struck off at a given time by the brain and purpose of man.[22]

Is it not literally true that it is only righteousness that exalteth a nation?

Some writers believe we are entering another dark age. The human brain has gone far toward conquering the domains of the atom and of space, but there has been no corresponding development of the human spirit. There is a widening abyss between material and moral progress.

And now atomic power has been linked with the immorality of communism.

It is reassuring to find that the foundation of the economic system of America is based upon righteousness. This is the source of our power and the last hope of civilization.

Said Abraham Lincoln:

> Even as we here hold the power and bear the responsibility, we shall nobly save or meanly lose the last best hope of earth.[23]

---

22 William E. Gladstone, quoted by John Bartlett (ed.), *Familiar Quotations* (Little, Brown & Co., Boston, 1937), p. 450.

23 Abraham Lincoln, Annual Message to Congress, December 1, 1862, quoted by Roy P. Basler (ed.), *The Collected Works of Abraham Lincoln* (Rutgers University Press, New Brunswick, New Jersey, 1953), Vol. V, p. 537.

ENDNOTES

I. A Land of Opportunity
* The rightness of slavery was generally accepted, however, and further development of the American society had to take place before the principles underlying the Constitution were applied in their fullness to the Negro.

Made in the USA
Middletown, DE
09 January 2016